Let's Play a Story

Let's Play a Story

By ELIZABETH ALLSTROM

ILLUSTRATED BY JANET SMALLEY

FRIENDSHIP PRESS
NEW YORK

The Bible verses quoted in the text are from
the Revised Standard Version of the Bible,
copyright 1946 and 1952.

First printing December 1957
Second printing September 1959
Third printing August 1961

LIBRARY OF CONGRESS CATALOG CARD NUMBER: 57-6170

With happy memories of

Jasmine, Fortunata, and Julia
Isidore, Santo, and Joe

whose unusual contributions and joyous
participation in my first story play
gave me courage to try the
second . . . and the third . . .

Contents

CONTENTS

The Story and the Storyteller

An old-time recipe for cooking hare begins with the admonition, "First, catch your hare." This underlying idea is practical and universal; its application for those who are about to adventure in playing a story is obvious: "First, find your story."

STORIES HAVE LONG BEEN IMPORTANT

Down through the ages, from the long ago to this very day, stories have been important. The storyteller has been welcomed by listeners of all ages. In ancient times he told his stories around the campfire, and children and grandchildren who heard them became, in their turn, the storytellers, and thus kept alive the traditions and history of their people.

In the Middle Ages, the storyteller traveled the highways and carried his stories to palace, cottage, and hovel. He was many things to many people: a news reporter recounting happenings in distant places, a teacher bringing culture and education to his listeners, an entertainer dramatizing his tale with appropriate pose and gesture, a preacher emphasizing the spiritual values of goodness, truth, beauty, and the triumph of right over wrong.

Whatever his story, the storyteller made the words come alive for his listeners. Through them they *felt* the story, as truly as if the mood had been created for them by the notes of a musician, they *saw* it as truly as if the pictured scene had been created for them by the brush of an artist.

Later, with the advent of printing, the ability to read became the prized possession of more and more people, who could then enjoy stories by themselves. Children, however, were not content to have only the stories they read. Their cry continued: "Tell us a story!" Aunt Mary, Mother, Father, grandparents became the storytellers and retold the folk tales, Bible stories, poems, songs, and family traditions remembered from their youth.

Today it is much the same. Books are plentiful for borrowing and for owning, yet boys and girls still request the spoken story. Parents, teachers at home, in day school, and church school use it often and discover the old truth anew: that stories continue to teach, to entertain, to inspire the children who hear them.

STORY MATERIAL IS ALWAYS AT HAND

Stories today, as in the long ago, may be spun out of anything and everything. They need not come from the pages of a book. Every day, in the ordinary and extraordinary business of living, stories happen to individuals—to boys, girls, parents, teachers—happy stories, sad ones, commonplace ones, lively, dull, and surprising ones. Almost every individual has the urge and the ability to tell them.

"I met Lucy on the corner by the grocery store, and the funniest thing happened. . . ."

"Mr. Copeland said our class would have a surprise, so when the knock came on the door . . ."

"After my operation . . ."

From such events in the lives of the friends they know, the children they teach, the guests who visit, the travelers who tell of distant places,

and from reports in newspapers and books, on radio and television, and particularly in the Bible, teachers find abundant and rich story material. And they discover that they may use this material in many ways and on many occasions at home, at school, at church.

RELIGIOUS AND MISSIONARY STORIES

A story may be called a *religious* story—no matter what the source, title, or content—whenever it achieves one or more of the following results: develops within the listener the desire to live at his best, lifts him to an appreciation of another person, challenges him to use his gifts in the service of others, causes him to wonder about the great mysteries that surround him and to recognize a purpose and plan in all life, informs him about God and Jesus and about people who have lived in godly ways, and inspires him with love for Jesus and a desire to follow him.

A story may be called a *missionary* story whenever it accomplishes one or more of the following purposes: causes the listener to feel close to people of other lands, to understand them better, to put himself in their place and to identify with them, to accept persons of all races and all beliefs as members with himself of God's family, and to commit himself to helping in his own way to bring health, education, knowledge, and, above all, the Christian gospel and its message of love to those who have not yet experienced them.

WHAT A GOOD STORY DOES

Whatever its source or its subject, a story that is good:

- Describes events so that they seem natural

- Presents characters so that they seem to be real people doing real things

- Makes the listeners or readers care about what happens to the story people

3

HOW A GOOD STORY IS PUT TOGETHER

Whatever its subject or its length, every good story is put together in the same way.

THERE IS A BEGINNING

- This introduces the "who."

- It reveals the "when" and "where."

- It gives a hint about a problem in the plot to come.

- It arouses curiosity about the solution of the problem. For example, "Once upon a time (when), there was a giant (who), and he lived in a house (where) that was built of firecrackers (arousing curiosity)."

THERE IS A BODY

- This presents the series of happenings to the "who."

- The happenings move in orderly fashion without distracting side issues.

- They move without any backtracking of sequence.

THERE IS A CLIMAX

- This brings a crisis in "who's" affairs.

- It discloses the solution of the problem.

THERE IS AN END

- This comes quickly.

- It tells briefly what happened to the "who."

- It accounts for all the issues raised in the plot.

THE STORY AND THE STORYTELLER

A STORY HAS MANY PURPOSES

A story may be used for many purposes; the right story at the right time can be an instrument of great potential. Children not only hear the story's words and enjoy them, they also absorb the message and make it their own. The story can:

- Provide pleasure and enjoyment
- Kindle the imagination
- Be an emotional outlet bringing release
- Give new knowledge
- Become an added resource to the regular unit study
- Project the listeners into another's life and problems
- Bring new appreciations, new insights, new understandings
- Help to change attitudes
- Help to set standards for behavior and to solve problems
- Direct action
- Lead to worship
- Lead to other activities

GUIDEPOSTS FOR FINDING THE RIGHT STORY

The storyteller needs not only to find a story, but the right story. He will recognize the right one if it is one that:

- Appeals to him and that makes him feel confident he can tell it convincingly and well
- Offers an interesting beginning that will immediately capture the listeners' interest

5

- Seems appropriate for the age group who will hear it
- Seems suitable for the particular occasion or purpose for which it will be used
- Has "quality," that is, the words and ideas in it have beauty and appropriateness
- Makes the learning vivid and memorable
- Meets a particular need

If a story does not immediately meet these requirements, the teller had better tuck it away until a later time—perhaps six months or two years from now—and search for another.

PREPARATION FOR TELLING THE STORY

Upon finding the appropriate story the storyteller prepares to share it with others.

LEARNING THE STORY

VISUALLY, by remembering how each paragraph appears on the printed page and repeating it idea by idea.

BY SOUND, by remembering the spoken words that describe the situations in which the story people move.

BY WRITING AN OUTLINE of the action sequences, then filling in the various details from memory.

BY MEMORIZING all or a part of the story. Often a feeling of confidence can be achieved by knowing by memory the entire first and last paragraphs (see Pitfalls, page 10).

Whatever way the storyteller learns the story, he tries to see and feel each story event imaginatively, in order to make it live for others.

THE STORY AND THE STORYTELLER

PRACTICING IT ALOUD

ONE PART AT A TIME, practicing telling each part of the story separately, learning each one well, then putting the several parts together in the regular sequence.

OVER A PERIOD OF TIME, extending the practice period over several days and thus avoiding last minute anxieties.

IN ANY PLACE, finding a pretend audience in the garden, in the kitchen, or wherever work or leisure time allows, even in bed before drifting off to sleep at night.

THE STORYTELLER'S TOOLS

Worker, artist, storyteller—each one must learn to handle and use certain tools in connection with his work. Some tools at first may seem simple to master, others difficult, still others quite impossible. Using them successfully usually depends on a willingness to try and try again and on a refusal to be discouraged.

Some of the storyteller's tools are:

SELF-CONFIDENCE

No one need disqualify himself as a storyteller because he feels he lacks the glamour of Mr. X, the poise of Mr. Y, or the know-how of Mr. Z. Each person has his own particular gift and will have his own way of presenting a story, which he will in time learn to develop so that it serves him best. Basic qualities are sincerity and good will and a warm, genuine, friendly relationship between the storyteller and his listeners.

VOICE

Every voice has three ranges—high, medium, low—and by varying the rhythm and pace of his spoken words the storyteller learns to give variety and color to his voice and to avoid a singsong or monotonous effect.

Pauses

Effective pauses may build suspense, indicate lapse of time, introduce a new thought. Such pauses give children an opportunity to catch up with the story's action, to think about the point just made, to anticipate the next action.

Choice of words

Action verbs help to determine when and where to use staccato or emphatic phrases. Descriptive words that suggest sound, taste, smell, etc. help to make vivid and clear the intended picture, as:

"He clomped up the stairs, eating a spicy, juicy, red apple."

Posture

Whether seated or standing, the storyteller needs to keep head and shoulders erect and at the same time to give the impression of being comfortable, relaxed, and at ease. If seated, he needs to be near the children's level and able to look directly at them. If standing, he needs to be free to move a step forward, backward, or to the side as seems natural, while continuing to look directly at the boys and girls.

Gestures

If gestures are used, they should seem natural and spontaneous to the person using them. They can never be "set," planned, or forced, since with each new telling the story itself is created anew, and the previously used gestures may no longer seem appropriate.

Facial expression

Through his own happy expression, the storyteller shares with his listeners his personal delight in the story and gives assurance of the pleasure and enjoyment that lie ahead. Once the story begins, he uses such expressions as frowns, smiles, twinkling eyes, a downcast glance to portray the moods of the story characters.

Time

This also belongs to the storyteller and should be adequate, whether the story is told by the fire at home, in a classroom at school, in a service of worship at church school, or in any other situation. Stories are not to be hurried nor is the storyteller to seem under pressure of time. If only a brief period is available for a story, it should be matched with a brief story.

PITFALLS

The storyteller must be ready to meet pitfalls that can lessen the effect of his story. Pitfalls may be avoided by awareness of them and preparation to meet them.

DISTRACTIONS

Sometimes the storyteller's shining pin, flowing scarf, swinging earrings, dangling beads become more fascinating to the listeners than the story itself. When these are left on the bureau at home they can create no problem.

A sudden noise outside or a door opening at the rear of the room to admit latecomers may direct the children's attention away from the story. When the storyteller takes no notice of such distractions, but continues without pause or interruption, perhaps lowering his voice temporarily, the listeners' attention usually is quickly regained.

FORGOTTEN INCIDENTS

When a paragraph or page of the story is omitted because of stage fright or loss of memory, the storyteller never betrays this fact to his listeners. As soon as possible he tucks in the omitted part or an abbreviated form of it, fitting it in as well as he can, as:

"Now I must tell you that all this time while Dumpkin was talking to the king, he knew that he . . ."

"Larry had not forgotten that in the morning he had seen . . ."

INCOMPLETE MEMORIZATION

To memorize a story word for word is one way of preparation that not only takes a lot of time, but carries its own pitfalls, since if the memory fails, floundering and panic may result.

A more comfortable and more dependable way is to memorize the sequence of actions and depend on one's own ability to fill in the remembered details. However, when stories are written in a definite and picturesque language all their own, such as "In the high and far off times, O Best Beloved, the elephant had no trunk," or when they contain poetic phrases or bits of song, to change these parts even by a single syllable would alter the mood and feeling of the story, and so such passages should be carefully memorized.

GIVING AWAY THE CLIMAX

When the storyteller in the first sentence or paragraph gives away the plot, he is likely to lose his listeners' interest. There is no need to pay attention further. The end of the story and its "point" are already known to the listeners!

"I will tell you now about Zachaeus. Few people liked him, but Jesus became his friend, and after that others also became his friends. Now Zachaeus was a little man, and one day he . . ."

"My story today is about a little boy's pet cat that ran away from home and never was seen again."

CONDESCENSION

"Talking down" to children negates the feeling of closeness that should exist between teller and listeners. Unconsciously the storyteller is assuming an air of superiority. Even though its cause may be shyness, the children are quick to sense it, and the full effect of the story is lost.

SENTIMENTALITY

Sentimentality is to be avoided, particularly with juniors. If the children laugh instead of being touched at what the teller feels is a tender part of the story, the effect is lost.

"So the dear little pussycat went pit-pat, pit-pat, up the stairs to his own sweet home and his own soft bed."

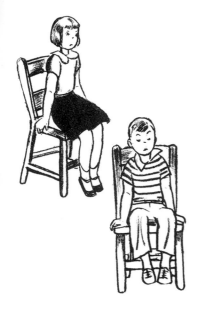

Such a story ending may suit kindergarten children but will sound silly to juniors.

Uncomfortable listeners

POOR SEATING ARRANGEMENT. If chairs are used, they need to be the proper size for the listeners. If children are seated on the floor, they must feel free to change their positions at will. A seven year old was quick to explain why he had not liked a particular story. "The bench was too big. When I made my feet touch the floor my back got tired. When I made my back touch, then my feet got tired; they wouldn't reach."

STUFFY AIR. A poorly ventilated room is equally discomforting for children. This condition often exists when the room has been unused for several days or has just been vacated by another group. Opening the windows a few minutes before the group enters is a good way to solve the problem.

TIRED CHILDREN. Another discomfort is fatigue. When children continue sitting for a story, after they already have been sitting for some time previous, they are likely to get restless. They should be given an opportunity to stand, walk about a little, or otherwise change position before the story begins.

THE STORY AND THE STORYTELLER

READING THE STORY VERSUS TELLING IT

Because of lack of time or lack of confidence a leader may prefer to read rather than to tell the story. Experience has shown that the story that is told has great advantages over the one that is read.

ADVANTAGES OF THE STORY THAT IS TOLD

The "told" story has a wonderful and magic quality to command and to hold the interest, particularly of larger groups, that the read story seldom has. The teller, freed from the pages of the book, can give all his attention to making the story come alive for the listeners.

It can join both leader and listeners in a way rarely achieved by the story that is read. The teller can look directly at the listeners and can come close to them.

It is more effective than the one that is read, usually. The exception is when a small group of younger children sit close beside the leader and while listening to the read story also look at and talk about the accompanying illustrations.

THE STORY THAT IS READ

Sometimes the story has to be read, because of a weak memory or lack of confidence on the part of the teller. Sometimes the reading of a story can be made into a step in learning to tell a story.

THE STORY READER NEEDS PREPARATION

Even in the read story, young listeners deserve the reader's best efforts. This "best" is not achieved by the leader's merely picking up the book and reading. Far from it! It comes when:

- The leader conscientiously has read and reread the text until every part of it is familiar

- The children see the reader's face lifted from the pages of the book frequently

- The pages are turned unobtrusively at the end of sentences rather than in the middle of them

- The story continues even while the children examine the illustrations

- The leader accurately pronounces unfamiliar and strange words and those written in another language

THE LISTENERS

FAMILY GROUPS

Many stories are enjoyed by all ages and are suitable for family listening. A feeling of closeness and fellowship prevails when a family listens to a story together, one member telling or reading it aloud. When such a practice becomes a permanent and looked-forward-to event in the family's weekly schedule, it brings a pleasure that is treasured as long as life itself.

CHILDREN'S GROUPS

Children, for the most part, prefer those stories that are within the understanding of their own age group and that have a special meaning for them. Every word need not be familiar; new words here and there help to build vocabularies, give spice and flavor, and provide elements of surprise. If their meaning is made apparent by the context of the sentence, they need no special explanation. Children understand many more spoken words than those they can read for themselves.

Children of the various age groups have special story needs and likings.

KINDERGARTEN children have a short interest span, so their stories need to be brief, told in short sentences, with frequent repetition of phrases and ideas. This group likes for-fun stories, those that describe children their own age, that relate family activities, that tell about animals and familiar

everyday objects. First person "I" stories usually are not as effective as those told in the third person.

PRIMARY children like story situations into which they can project themselves, those in which people practice the spiritual values of love, kindness, thoughtfulness of others. They are happy when the story words are descriptive, colorful, whimsical, even made up. Sensory words and phrases relating to touch, smell, taste, sight, and hearing also have a particular place in primary stories. One group of seven year olds described their story likes as follows:

"It's got to make sense."

"And be simple-ized—not a lot of things you don't need."

"I get jittery if it's too long."

"I want to feel how the story person is—sad or mad or glad, then I *am* him."

JUNIOR boys and girls are active, curious, hero loving, patriotic, fond of humor, so their stories need to contain these qualities. They like realistic stories, ones that are placed in a specific place and in a specific time. Among their wide range of story interests are those that:

- Describe the wonders of the world in which they live
- Make real the heroes of the past and present
- Tell about life in the air, on the earth, and in the sea
- Relate to family, home, country

Juniors enjoy the day-by-day or week-by-week serials that are entertaining and informative.

AND CHILDREN OF ALL AGES LIKE THOSE STORIES THEY CAN PLAY!

2

Playing the Story

WHY PLAY A STORY

There are values to be found in story playing that cannot be gained by any other method of teaching. Here are some of the most important.

FIRST AND FOREMOST

Playing a story can be an important educational factor in a child's development: It helps him to learn, grow, develop, change. Teachers in day school and church school now recognize story play as an integral part of their teaching program and find ways to use it quite as freely and as often as they use music, crafts, and other creative activities. They no longer consider it as "extra" or a "waste of time."

SOME OTHER REASONS

- Children have fun playing a story. It gives satisfaction to the individual; it adds joy to group adventure.

- It opens the heart in appreciation of others different from oneself.

- It widens horizons, as mind, spirit, and good will stretch out to include people of other times and places.

PLAYING THE STORY

- In story play the child forgets himself. To play the part of another person, even for a brief period, brings an understanding of him and his situation as no amount of reading can do. The "actor" can absorb the story character's desirable traits and be inspired by them.

- It brings an appreciation of the creative spirit in others.

- It enriches a study unit and makes it come alive.

- It is a means of easing tensions. *Physical* tensions are released through movement and activity; *emotional* and *mental* tensions are released through new accomplishments; *emotional* reactions against others become less frequent and less intense when all members of the group are working happily together.

- It is a means of finding out why people behave as they do.

- It provides the teacher with an immediate and first-hand opportunity to know the children better: the bossy one, the irresponsible one, the show-off, the natural leader, the dependable one, the "I can't" and the "Let me" ones.

WHEN TO PLAY A STORY

The time to play a story is immediately after the children have had a story experience worthy of being continued. Such a story may be found on the pages of a book or it may be found in a class experience, such as taking a trip, entertaining a visitor, seeing a filmstrip, learning a song, studying a picture, observing a pet animal. Always it gives added interest to the lesson study, supplementing and enriching it.

The teacher, in selecting the story from a book or in providing the enriching experience, usually has already anticipated in imagination its dramatic possibilities and presents the material in a way to awaken the children to these possibilities so that dramatization follows naturally.

When this occurs, children who know from experience that playing a story is a satisfying way of translating into action something that has interested them will exclaim, "Let's play a story!" When lack of experience makes such suggestions unlikely, the teacher will initiate the idea and follow it through. In either case children and teacher soon discover that their classroom is a stage, that they are the happy actors upon it, and that their story is about to be enjoyed in a new and different way.

WAYS TO PLAY A STORY

There is no one way that is the right way to play a story. There are many ways, but in whatever way the story is played it always expresses what the children have learned.

A SIMPLE WAY

The spontaneous pantomime play of younger children is one of the simplest ways of playing a story. It can be played on the spur of the moment and for their own immediate enjoyment. They have no thought of repeating it in the same way on another occasion, no thought of playing it for others to see.

AN ELABORATE WAY

Older boys and girls are able to play a story in a more elaborate way and usually desire to do so. Their story play

18

PLAYING THE STORY

may be entirely created and acted by themselves. They may plan the scenes and the dialogue and also any scenery and costumes that are desired. They may portray the various story characters and assume all the responsibilities for the play's success. Such a play sometimes may be shared with an audience of other children, parents, or both.

SOME IN-BETWEEN WAYS

The following ways of playing a story are neither "too hard" nor "too easy." Each leader will recognize which ones are within the interests and abilities of his group.

PANTOMIME: The children become the characters and act out the story incidents, while the teacher narrates the story.

TABLEAUX: The children pose a story incident without movement or words.

PICTURES: The children present the story by means of their own colored drawings or paintings.

PUPPETS: The story is related through the actions and speech of puppets or figures the children have made from clay, cardboard, or clothespins.

RHYTHMS: The story's words and mood are interpreted through rhythmic motions with or without music.

READING: The story is read aloud, one child reading the connecting narrative lines, each of the others reading the lines of a particular character.

WAYS THE PLAY DIFFERS FROM THE STORY

Whether the story is played by means of pantomime, puppets, or real "actors," it never can be an exact reproduction of the story itself, because:

• The story tells what happened, the play shows the events happening.

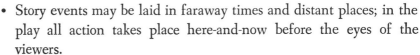

- Story events may be laid in faraway times and distant places; in the play all action takes place here-and-now before the eyes of the viewers.

- The story describes a character's feelings; in the play the character expresses his own feelings.

- The story's action may cover a period of one day, two weeks, one hundred years; in the play it must be condensed to fit into a short space of time.

CHILDREN WHO PLAY THE STORY

KINDERGARTEN

Children of this age group emphasize their playing rather than the story that is played, and for their playing they need open and uncluttered spaces and plenty of time. They are not to be hurried. Ideas and suggestions for creative action do not come from this age group immediately on "pushing the button," nor do their responses often come at the teacher's first invitation.

Kindergarten story play is likely to be more successful early in the session rather than toward the close. At this time the children usually are rested, responsive, and eager to enter into whatever is presented, and the activity may proceed in leisurely fashion.

There are many starting points for story play—the weather, a child's adventure, a Bible verse—and the teacher suggests one in conversation, usually without preliminaries, as for instance:

"Whoo-ooo! The strong wind this morning blew Jim down his steps and along the pavement to church school. Show us, Jim, how it blew you. . . . Now it is blowing all of us! Hold your caps . . . tie on your hats. . . ."

When kindergarten children play a story they enjoy being members of the larger group, yet each one likes to do the part of the story play that captures his fancy, each one becoming the wind, the child Miriam, the postman, the slow, crawling turtle as he chooses. One child starts, the others follow or not, as they like. There usually will be imitation, but the child is free to create action according to his fancy.

A kindergarten child is seldom concerned with the form of his acting; he does it in the way that brings satisfaction to himself. He will improvise appropriate action if the leader pauses in the narration and glances at him expectantly. He does not learn set speeches, yet he can fill in short phrases or impromptu sentences of dialogue if the narrator stops and waits for him to do so. And usually he can correlate his actions with his spoken words.

Five year olds readily imagine scenery and costumes. Real ones are not necessary, although children of this age like to "dress up" and can improvise what is needed from whatever is at hand. Their interest span is short. When playing alone, a five year old may be a father eating breakfast, a bear at the zoo, Superman flying through space, or a train running the tracks, in quick succession.

PRIMARY

Children of primary age have no hesitancy in creating a play. They are readily able to transform any of their story experiences into dramatic form. Sometimes their story play is for-the-moment only, fun for themselves; at other times they want to put time, thought, and extra work on their play and share it with friends. Each type of dramatic play has its own contribution to make to the children's development.

Each child likes to portray a particular character and to do it in his own way, but he wants that character to be a part of the complete story scene. He likes to play stories other than those for his own age group, particularly those for children younger than himself.

Primary plays must present the concrete, not the abstract, showing a character *doing* the friendly deed, not merely *telling about* doing it. The

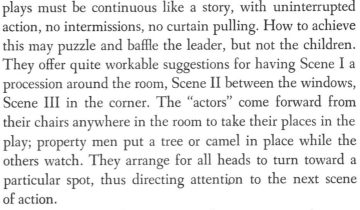

plays must be continuous like a story, with uninterrupted action, no intermissions, no curtain pulling. How to achieve this may puzzle and baffle the leader, but not the children. They offer quite workable suggestions for having Scene I a procession around the room, Scene II between the windows, Scene III in the corner. The "actors" come forward from their chairs anywhere in the room to take their places in the play; property men put a tree or camel in place while the others watch. They arrange for all heads to turn toward a particular spot, thus directing attention to the next scene of action.

The teacher with preconceived notions may discover, when taught by primary children, that it makes sense to expand the play's action from a limited and set space to all parts of the room, that the informal approach to actors and scenery permits freer interpretation of the characters, and that this way is more fun for everybody, including himself. He ends up preferring to work in this manner.

Lengthy rehearsals are not for primary children. Spontaneity and interest diminish and may be lost entirely if practice periods are too numerous. The children need to get the idea for the play, plan how to develop it, practice it a couple of times, and give it!

PLAYING THE STORY

JUNIOR

Boys and girls of junior age prefer plays that are like their favorite stories, having:

- A plot with plenty of action

- An interesting leading character who is engaged in unusual and exciting activities

- A message worth remembering

Because of their added years, filled with deeper insight, broader experiences, and greater appreciation of people and events, juniors can greatly enrich any story they choose to play. They understand the creative approach to drama and readily develop dialogue, plan action, and offer a variety of ideas for costumes and scenery. This age group can quickly bring a story to life and many times do so in the classroom for their own pleasure. If the play is to be shared with others, the juniors will work earnestly to make it a worthy presentation and will assume willingly extra responsibilities, such as looking up information in the family encyclopedia and bringing materials from home.

Juniors can sustain enthusiasm for a play over several sessions, but their practices need to be brief and to the point, lest the children tire of the business at hand and discover the possibilities of wrapping themselves inside the folds of the stage curtains or hiding behind the piano.

Each junior likes to take the part of one particular character, though at one practice or another he eventually may have a turn to play every part. When the class, or a committee representing it, writes the dialogue lines that are the basis of the play, these lines may be typed and a copy given to each person. Sometimes a prepared script of this sort saves time and gives security to the less confident actors. However, most juniors are quick to absorb the play's message, soon pick up lines of others, and often can slip into another's role if that person should fail at the last minute.

23

Juniors are able to evaluate their work honestly and usually can accept criticism from others in the same spirit. Being perfectionists, they may desire a more elaborate play than is possible within the time limit, but they usually are amenable to discussion and compromise.

WHAT STORY TO PLAY

Not every story the leader reads or tells is suitable for dramatization. Important requirements for the story-about-to-be-played are:

A BASIC PLOT, easy to outline, easy to picture, easy to transfer into action and dialogue; one that is interesting to children and that proceeds logically from a stimulating start to an exciting climax and satisfying ending. The story should have few or no narrative passages because these cannot be easily transferred into dialogue and action.

STORY CHARACTERS that go places, do things, and converse with one another in direct discourse.

A MESSAGE worthy of remembering and of sharing with others; one that will assure an attitude of good will.

AN ACCURATE AND TRUE PICTURE of the described situation, especially when the situation concerns people and customs of another land.

USES FOR THE STORY PLAY

Story play may begin in different ways (see following chapter). It also may "end" in varied, unusual, and even unexpected ways as shown by the following examples:

IN WORSHIP

One kindergarten group played the story of the Indian Corn Dance in rhythmic movements and upon discovering it to be related to Thanksgiving, included the song in their Thanksgiving service of worship.

PLAYING THE STORY

IN FURTHER STUDY

A third grade group dramatized a Christmas carol from India and through it became curious about other customs and activities of boys and girls in India. Through an exchange of letters, pictures, and gifts, they became friends with a group of Indian children. Later they invited an American missionary returned from India to visit them, sought information about ways their church works in India, and succeeded in finding a way themselves to help in the work.

IN A GIFT

A primary group, invited to spend an afternoon visiting blind children in their school, decided that a play would be the most appropriate gift for the new friends. It would not wear out, could not be lost or broken, could not be eaten and thus forgotten. It could "go around" for everyone and would perhaps be long remembered by children and teachers alike. With contagious enthusiasm they set about preparing their gift in a way to make it live for children who would see it through the mediums they knew best—hearing it with their ears, feeling it with their hands.

IN A SUMMARY

Junior boys and girls discovered that a surprising number of the games they played, vegetables they ate, pretty articles they owned or had seen, names of towns, rivers, and states they had visited or studied about were actually gifts from the first Americans, the Indians. Their discovery moved them to put this new knowledge into a play to share with others.

THE GUEST AUDIENCE

IT IS NEVER ESSENTIAL

The first concern in playing a story is the growth and development of the children. Creative dramatics has no concern that children become "actors," nor that story plays be created for a guest audience. In fact, such audiences are of secondary importance; in some instances they may even hinder the children's growth by emphasizing the "actors" too much and the process of creating the play too little. The greatest values of a story play might easily be lost if every story played by children ended up in front of an audience—other than that made up of members of the group itself.

WHEN THERE IS ONE

At times a primary or junior group may want to share their group-created play with other children or parents. Always the emphasis is on the sharing of an experience that has excited the children—not on the people who are invited to share it. Such occasions are special ones, and the players often want to add the extras of simple scenery and costumes. Such touches are fun to create and fun to use, but they are not needed in presenting the story play's message, nor are they intended to be a substitute for imagination.

FOR THE LEADER AND AUDIENCE TO REMEMBER

Never, no NEVER, is the story play to be thought of or spoken of as a "performance" or "production."

REMINDERS FOR THE LEADER

Whatever story is selected for playing, whatever way is chosen to play it, the following reminders may be helpful for the leader as he prepares, plans, practices, and participates with his group in this activity:

PLAYING THE STORY

- Know the children and materials equally well and try to put them together in the best possible way.

- Prepare adequately. When the teacher is prepared the children do their most creative work.

- Be ready to offer suggestions and also to receive them.

- Avoid telling what to do and how to do it.

- Avoid letting the child see or hear anything that could give him a pattern.

- Make no decisions in advance. Story play is a "we" process with ideas contributed from both leader and children.

- Always encourage the participation of the timid child, but never force it.

- Remember that a not-so-good play, created with happy participation from all the children, is more to be desired than a much better one created with drudgery and driving by a determined teacher.

- Do not expect perfection, because what is done perfectly is not childlike.

- Briefly review the details of the play at each session: children cannot remember them for a lengthy time between practices.

- If the story play is being shared with others, practice it at least once in the place where it will be given at that time.

- Learn from Shakespeare: "No profit grows where is no pleasure ta'en." This applies to children and teacher alike.

3

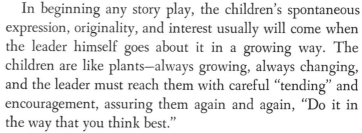

First Steps in Story Play

WAYS TO BEGIN

In beginning any story play, the children's spontaneous expression, originality, and interest usually will come when the leader himself goes about it in a growing way. The children are like plants—always growing, always changing, and the leader must reach them with careful "tending" and encouragement, assuring them again and again, "Do it in the way that you think best."

The method the leader uses to begin a story will depend upon the situation and experience of the children.

WHEN THE CHILDREN ARE IN A FREE SITUATION

To begin story play with KINDERGARTEN and YOUNGER PRIMARY children is seldom a problem. They like to play and usually are ready to do so, as a part of their natural action. What they play every day is as real to them as the world in which they live.

On the spot and without preliminary practice they eagerly become their Christmas toys: a jump up jack-in-the-box, a bouncing ball, smooth sliding ice skates, a clown doll. They assume the parts of favorite story characters: Tinkerbell,

28

FIRST STEPS IN STORY PLAY

Pinocchio, Bashful, and the real-life characters of Mother, the family doctor, the train engineer, the postman, the teacher, the milkman.

Theirs is a free kind of play that is spontaneous and for fun, and it may originate from their own idea or the teacher's. There is no thought except the immediate pleasure of the players.

OLDER BOYS AND GIRLS who are in a "free" class situation likewise have little trouble about beginning a play. They probably are accustomed to presenting their own ideas, hearing and evaluating ideas of others, and putting the best ones into use. Such children are seldom at a loss for ways to begin; for them the play immediately becomes a "we" project with each person offering what he can. This co-operative planning continues through each step of the play making.

WHEN THE STORY PLAY IDEA IS NEW

Where boys and girls are accustomed to a stereotyped class procedure, the teacher may find some of them tense, self-conscious, awkward, shy. Especially is this true if their only dramatic experience has been reciting lines from memory and trying to imitate a movie personality. If children have never been challenged to depart from the usual, to adventure into the untried, their response to the invitation "Let's play a story" may be giggles, silliness, reluctance, perhaps hostility.

Therefore, the wise teacher does not present the idea to them abruptly with a direct question, as "Would you like to be in a play?" Such an approach often openly invites a

loudly chorused "NO!" or a stubborn silence. Instead, he tries a positive, confident statement that assumes interested co-operation and offers a suggestion for action in a familiar area, as "The father is late for work. Show us how he runs for the bus." "The player on first base is going to steal second. Show us how."

Then, referring to the story to be played, "Ronny, your voice is good for a father's. You be the father and choose someone to be your son. The conversation you will have will be about the surprise you are planning for Mother."

Expecting creative responses from the players, the teacher is not disappointed. Almost before the boys know how it comes about, they have assumed their parts, and the story has begun.

"That was fine," the teacher encourages. "Each of you made your actions convincing and true. Joe, this time you try the son's part and choose someone for your father. . . ."

Then, "Who has an idea how the mother feels and what she would say? All right, Sue, you almost overhear the secret that is being planned for you."

In participation such as this the children gradually become less inhibited and begin to move and act in response to an inner emotion. Those who at first gave little or no response will see how much fun the others are having and will want to join in.

Lack of previous experience in story play is no reason for being satisfied with less than one's best efforts. There is no place for consoling excuses such as:

"So what if we did things wrong! It's our first time!"

"Oh, it doesn't matter how we did it. No one saw us."

"It was a change for the children anyhow."

If children are to gain from the story play experience, they need to have a feeling of accomplishment, to be happy in having done their best, and to want to try the adventure again.

FIRST STEPS IN STORY PLAY

PREPARATION

Preparation is whatever the teacher does to get ready for his teaching, such as keeping himself rested and alert, collecting the tangible materials needed for his group, searching for ideas in his own mind and in books.

THE TEACHER IS ALWAYS READY

To the prepared teacher, the children's request "Let's play a story" never is unwelcome. Sometimes it may be baffling, as when after a visitor's account of watching a spider spin its strong, fragile web, the children exclaimed, "Let's spin webs!" But it was not baffling to them. "Play us some spinning music," they asked their friend at the piano, and in rhythms they enacted the wondrous scene.

The request sometimes may seem to present insurmountable difficulties, as when after hearing the story of a migrant family whose truck broke down on their way to "peaches," the children exclaimed, "Let's be the family riding in the truck!" In the children's minds, there were no difficulties. With a large sheet of paper, colored paints, and long handled

brushes they soon created their truck, adding painted brooms, pots, and pans across the top (see Properties, page 51). Mother and children sat behind the cutout windows, Father held the steering wheel in realistic fashion, and soon the happy family were on their way, watching the fields they passed and talking about what they would find when they reached the peach orchards.

Sometimes the request may seem even quite impossible, as when one group insisted, "Oh, yes, let's be the skeptics heckling Galileo when he tries to prove to them that falling objects of different weights fall at the same rate of speed." And they painted the leaning tower of Pisa and arranged a ladder back of it so that Galileo seemed to stand on the balcony high above, and the children became the skeptics on the ground below, as the class played the story of this famous tradition.

Let no teacher feel afraid. Children work out their stories in their own way, even ones that may seem difficult, even Moses listening on the mountain and returning to tell his people of God's commandments; and the rich young ruler after leaving Jesus, going on his way, paying no attention to the lame man needing his help.

THE TEACHER USES EVERY IDEA

Whatever the story to be played, the teacher tries to anticipate the children's moods, responses, manner of participation, then seeks to encourage their ideas about what to do. He uses the ideas contributed as seems best—some immediately and some later, finding an appropriate place for each one and neglecting no idea that has been shared in good faith.

FIRST STEPS IN STORY PLAY

MOTIVATION

Motivation is the plan the teacher develops to stimulate the children's interest in the project about to be undertaken and to establish the mood so they will eagerly participate in the project. From the many possible ways of motivating story play, one successful example for each age group is described below.

THROUGH A GAME—Kindergarten

THE TEACHER BEGINS IT. After telling a story about a familiar neighborhood helper, the teacher may stimulate the children's interest in story play through a sort of game. "What neighbor helped me?"

Going to the door the teacher pretends to pull a market cart into the room. He stops at a nearby table to unpack the pretend groceries. "Everything looked so good today I bought enough to fill my cart . . . oranges . . . cereal . . ."

At the children's cry, "The grocer at the store helped you!" the teacher asks, "What shall I do with my purchases?"

THE CHILDREN JOIN IN THE FUN. The children match their responses with action, each locating a pretend place and putting a pretend package there, as:

"Oh, here's the icebox. I'll put the milk away."
"I'll put the cookies in this jar."
"I'll put the cereal on the shelf," etc.

The teacher acknowledges this help and continues, "Now each of you may choose from my packages something to eat that you especially like. Who can guess what James chose? I think he has a banana."

James may accept this clue and begin to peel his banana, or he may object, "It isn't a banana. It's cornflakes."

33

The conversation continues accordingly: "Here's a saucer. Here's a spoon. Get the milk from the icebox."

THE STORY PLAY IS EXTENDED. At the second playing, further action may be suggested: "The rest of your family must also be hungry. If you put more cups and saucers on the table, Grandmother and your brother may come and eat with you."

FURTHER PLAY IS ANTICIPATED. When the children leave at the close of the session, the idea of continued play may be presented: "Some neighborhood helper is sure to help you this week. Watch and see and be ready to show us, and we will try to guess which one it is."

THROUGH WELL PLANNED QUESTIONS—Primary

Following a story from the unit "Making Friends at Church," the teacher's planned questions may start the children's pantomime play.

"Where does Lois' family live?"
"How can you make this place seem like a real home?"
"Who are the other members of this family?"
"Where will the neighbor family live?"
"Who belongs to it?"
"What does Rodney do when Lois stops to visit?"
"Where will the church be?"
"How will the families know it is a friendly place?"
"How will the minister welcome everyone?"

THE CHILDREN RESPOND WITH ACTION. As ideas come to them, the children go from place to place in the room to demonstrate them.

"The family could live here in this corner."
"This table could be the stove, see? And this one the piano."
"Molly could be the mother and choose the others for her family."

"The neighbor family can live in the other corner."

"The church is here by the window."

"Two people could swing their arms high and be the bell calling everybody to come and worship."

"The minister would shake hands with people like this. . . ."

THE STORY PANTOMIME. After the children's ideas indicate the what, where, how, and who of the action, the teacher directs, "Each actor will take his place. . . . Scene I in Lois' home; Scene II in the neighbor's home; Scene III in the church. As I retell the story you do at the proper time whatever action seems natural to the character you play. Make it seem as real as you can. The words of the story will give you the clues that you need."

Through reading aloud—Juniors

An effective way to whet the juniors' appetites for story play is to suggest their reading aloud exciting or meaningful passages from appropriate and well chosen stories related to the current study.

CHOOSING THE STORY. The chosen story or selection may be humorous or sad, new or familiar, but it should provide reading parts for each member of the group. The dialogue needs to be simple, without difficult phrases or hard-to-pronounce words. Story characters should be those whose voice inflections are easily copied by children.

ARRANGEMENT OF ACTORS. For the reading the children are seated comfortably around a table, the seating order being unimportant. Each reader has on the table in front of him an identical copy of the text and reads his lines from it, turning the pages quietly and focusing his full attention on the printed words. If the table is in the center of the room and the "audience" seated on all sides surrounding it, the story play becomes a kind of "theater in the round" (see Chapter 9).

WHO DOES WHAT. One member of the group may act as announcer and give the title of the story that is to be presented and briefly explain why it is being shared.

Another's part may be to read aloud the narrative lines that bind the story together. They are important and need to be read with meaning and understanding.

Others choose a particular story character to interpret, trying to express by voice and facial expression his moods of joy, surprise, curiosity, dismay, fear.

AUDIENCE PARTICIPATION. A variation of the reading technique is to divide the group, some acting as readers as suggested above, and the remainder becoming the "audience." At an exciting point or climax in the story, the reading stops, and the audience is requested to suggest a possible outcome for the story. If a problem is involved, several solutions may be offered. The listeners then decide, in the light of Christian principles, which solution seems best and why. This solution may be accepted as the story's final ending, or the readers may present the ending as given in the story.

STORIES SUITABLE FOR READING ALOUD
   Girls: "The Witch Doctor's Daughter," from *Many Hands in Many Lands*
   Boys: "Zuka Changes His Mind," from *The Missionary Story Hour*
   Girls and Boys: "Good-by to the Ozarks," from *Blueberry Acres*

DIFFICULTIES AND HOW TO MEET THEM

No matter how experienced the leader, difficulties of many sorts put in their appearance from time to time, often to be followed by the avowal "I'll just never try dramatics with my group again." Realizing that others also have difficulties may be one kind of consolation, but knowing how to handle the difficulties that appear is the real help.

FIRST STEPS IN STORY PLAY

THE TEACHER'S FEELING OF FAILURE

Discouragement comes at some time to teachers of all age groups, and it comes in spite of good preparation and motivation. In an honest search for the cause, the teacher may discover that he is attempting to measure the play's results by his own adult standard of perfection rather than by the children's enjoyment and participation. Or that he has chosen the story play at random, without seeking the children's opinions and suggestions. Or even that in his haste to play a story he has taken the first one that came into his hands, only to discover later that it had no immediate interest or reality for the group. However, one, two, or even three discouraging experiences need not be the cause for quitting.

CHILDREN'S REFUSAL TO CO-OPERATE

Disappointment and disillusionment may await the leader of OLDER PRIMARIES and JUNIORS, when his suggestions to them are met with silly replies, inattention, rude interruptions, or refusal to co-operate.

Actually, such troublemakers probably are eager to participate in the group's project, but are too embarrassed to do so. They want to be included, yet do not quite know how to show a matter-of-fact interest.

To recognize each such child as a needed member of the group and to offer him a specific responsibility challenges and holds his interest, as for example:

"The play must not run over twenty minutes. Please watch the time for us."

"Each speaker's voice must be heard distinctly. Please sit near the back and raise your hand if there is a word that is not clear."

"The illustrations in this book may suggest ideas for improving the play. In the discussion period, you may tell us what you discovered."

RIDICULE FOR AN ACTOR

If humiliating jibes or derisive laughter are hurled by some child at an unusually self-conscious actor or one who is easily embarrassed, the teacher may meet the situation by ignoring this behavior and immediately offering to the actor words of honest praise for the part he has played, which will express to all within sight and sound his own confidence in him.

THE SHY CHILD

The shy child who prefers to observe rather than to participate in story play probably appears more often among older rather than younger children. It is not always lack of interest that prevents him from joining in. Often he shows noticeable interest and seems quite willing to help with plans, but whenever acting is mentioned, he quietly withdraws. Such a child may be afraid of failure, of making a mistake, of being laughed at, of attempting anything new, or—he just may not want to act! Sometimes he resorts to reading a book during story play time and ignores even his best friend's request, "Come on, we need you." Sometimes he just sits on the sidelines and watches silently what his classmates are doing.

The teacher never gives up trying to make the activity appealing. At each refusal he suggests a way the shy child may help, but he never threatens or uses force to gain co-operation. He is patient, patient, patient.

38

FIRST STEPS IN STORY PLAY

For three years in the primary department shy Deborah refused all invitations to participate in story play. Then one day in the fourth grade when she was offered a tambourine to become one of the maidens of the Egyptian princess, she accepted it. Seriously, gracefully, she danced with the others the Song of Joy when they discovered the baby at the water's edge. When the next role was offered, Deborah eagerly took part.

STEPS IN PLANNING A STORY PLAY

When a story play becomes more than a for-fun activity and is planned seriously, perhaps for sharing with others, more detailed preparation and practice are usually involved. Yet the "we" process of planning continues. With older primaries and juniors an outline something like the following may be put on the blackboard to become a reminder of the needed planning. At other times such steps may be only in the leader's mind. Details as contributed by the group are filled in under each heading and used for immediate or future reference.

In the outline here presented, the key question to be asked of the group by the leader is indicated in each step of the process, as well as the reasons for it and some procedures that may develop from it.

PURPOSE
"What is the play's message?"

Every play, like every story, has a message. Each actor must know this message, for he cannot convincingly convey to others something that is only hazy and indefinite to himself. The purpose is stated simply and in a few words, as:

- To tell about Dr. Lewis and his missionary airplane
- To introduce Elena, who lives in the Philippine Islands
- To present the life of a Hebrew family in ancient Palestine
- To make people laugh

SCENES

"What scenes seem necessary to tell the message in the most interesting way?"

Children have no hesitancy in suggesting four, five, six scenes for their play, but when each scene is considered along with the question "Does it help to tell the message?" they soon are able to evaluate which do and which do not. No matter how exciting a scene may seem, unless it helps to move the plot along it should not be included.

CHARACTERS

"What people are needed in Scene I? In Scene II?"

Children often want to include all the characters in the story. They can see that this is impractical as they discover inadequate stage space, the obvious confusion of too many characters, and the likelihood of obscuring the message of the play.

Many characters are played with equal effect by boys or girls. Primary boys and girls may be grain growing in the farmer's field or guards of the king's palace, a junior girl may be the lad Moses, a junior boy may speak the lines of an "old woman."

A character not in the story often is added to the play for interest, for emphasis, or to provide an extra part, such as a tumbling clown, a child who always asks questions, an announcer.

OTHER RESPONSIBILITIES

"Acting is only one responsibility of the play. What are some of the others?"

Not every play offers a speaking or acting part for each member of the group. This is no detriment, since not every child wants such a part. When children look ahead in their planning and see the possible jobs needed to make their play a success, they usually know their own and their friends' choices, as:

- Planning the dialogue
- Helping with costumes and properties
- Creating the scenery
- Making announcement posters
- Welcoming any guests who come to the play

The teacher, knowing the group and their needs, tries to arrange the various responsibilities so that each child makes his personal contribution in a way that brings personal satisfaction and a feeling of accomplishment. No matter how small the job, each child should have one, should find pleasure in it, and should obtain a moderate degree of skill in it. When the teacher feels that a child has held back voluntarily or has not been chosen for a part and needs a particular experience within the play, he usually can find a way to bring participation about without seeming to do so.

PRACTICING

"Who will try the neighbor's part?"

Some children will offer at once. Others may be persuaded to try when a classmate suggests they can do it well. Children know one another's assets and limitations and usually are honest in their appraisal of them. Before long it becomes obvious where each one seems to fit best, doing the part that suits him best.

Each child needs an opportunity to practice being more than one character. When each child knows the story well, helps to plan the action and dialogue, and lives the story people during the practice periods, this becomes a simple matter. The advantage is obvious, since no postponement of the play is necessary should bad weather, illness, a faulty alarm clock, or an unexpected trip to Grandmother's remove a key character on the day the play is to be given. The children present are well able to carry on.

ACTION AND DIALOGUE

"How does the father let us know his feelings about the trouble that has come to them?"

"What does the mother do?"

When a child steps aside as himself and lends the story character his body and voice, he partially becomes that person. It is helpful to know something about the character's age, temperament, build, occupation, place in the family group. When the child takes on the character's inner feelings and thoughts he becomes that person in a very real way, for these "inside feelings" affect not only his spoken words, bodily movement, and facial expression, but also his entire personality.

If the character is in general a jovial, easygoing fellow, what makes him that way? How does this show through in what he does and says as differing from the continually tired, grumpy sort of person? The actor needs to know.

42

FIRST STEPS IN STORY PLAY

Story play dialogue attempts to be true to life, yet it is more condensed than real life dialogue. Its short sentences sustain interest, give punch, and are more effective. Some sentences are used exactly as they appear in the story, but most are rephrased in the children's own words. First lines need to capture interest; subsequent ones permit dialogue to unfold as in a good story, showing what happens to the "who," then moving on to the exciting climax and the satisfying ending.

COSTUMES AND SCENERY (See also Chapter 4)

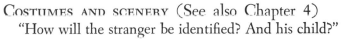

"How will the stranger be identified? And his child?"

Costumes and scenery are never essential for a play's success. Both can readily be imagined. If used, children will plan and create them; elaborate ones are always to be discouraged.

Simple, effective costumes may be created from materials at hand—a piece of cloth worn cape fashion across the shoulders or wrapped turban fashion around the head of a primary child often adds to the make-believe of putting himself into another's place and may permit playing the part with more conviction.

Juniors have a real interest in costumes and will probably ask to have them whenever possible, especially for those plays that may be shared with others. Being in costume, even a simple one, often helps a junior to forget himself. And costumes, many juniors feel, lend dignity and importance to their play.

Scenery, though merely suggested, is also fun, and making it often provides an interest for those children who refuse a speaking part.

43

EVALUATION

"If we play this story again, what have we learned that will help us?"

Good as well as not so good points are to be considered in the evaluation. Even though the play is not to be repeated, evaluate it as if it were. A thoughtfully expressed opinion is of more value than a hasty "yes" or "no," so questions need to be carefully phrased, as:

"Why are you so certain the visiting group understood the play's message?"

"Why have we enjoyed working so hard?"

"What are your reasons for wanting to omit Scene III?"

Individual criticism is kept impersonal and objective by using the story character's name, "Dr. Smith," rather than the child's actual name, "Dick," as:

"What happened when Dr. Smith got out of character and looked out at the visitors?"

"Why did Mrs. Smith's conversation seem so true to life?"

"How did David Smith hold everyone's interest?"

The teacher's evaluation of the play is based not on unimportant details, such as whether or not the lines were remembered, the dialogue heard, or the scene realistic, but rather on what happened to the children during the period of preparation for the play. Has the experience helped each one of them to:

- Assume responsibility for his own behavior

- Accept group decisions

- Change attitudes

- Strengthen old friendships and make new ones

- Develop new interests

- Absorb new information

44

4

Settings and Properties

SETTINGS

Settings are not even thought of when KINDERGARTEN children play a story. When OLDER CHILDREN suggest that it would be fun to have "a throne for the king" or to show "the bean vines in the field," such scenes may be achieved without folderol, costly supplies, complicated head work, or hours of time.

Special knowledge on how to achieve them is not required. Almost any teacher already has or can secure the needed items: large sheets of paper, poster paints, long handled brushes, scissors, thumbtacks, masking tape. The children provide ideas and the eagerness to begin. Together (if the teacher is not inwardly rebelling, "We haven't time to fuss with all this"), they can transform even the most unlikely spot in their classroom into the deck of a sailing ship or a humble home in Palestine.

SIMPLE SETTINGS ARE EFFECTIVE

Simple settings are more desirable than elaborate ones, a mere suggestion often being more rewarding than too much detail. When the setting is too real it seems artificial,

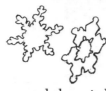

and there is little reason to stretch imaginations; every story play needs imagination!

THE SEASONS. Large and small lacy snowflakes cut from newsprint and pinned hit or miss fashion to a black background present a winter scene of beauty. Leaves drawn freehand by the children on large sheets of paper, painted red, yellow, brown, cut out, and pinned against the background indicate fall in a colorful way.

MUSIC. Notes—large, small, middle-sized, sixteenths, quarters, halves—drawn in oversized shapes by the children and painted in bright colors, cut out, and pinned to the background curtain, immediately establish the mood for a play about music.

GIFTS FOR OTHERS. When their gifts for others are the subject of children's story play, appropriate reminders may be placed against the curtain to become striking and original backgrounds, as:
The children's own painted *illustrations of the actual gifts:* towels, washcloths, toothbrushes, toothpaste, soap
Bright replicas of their own *hands, which made the gifts,* traced on paper, colored, and cut out
Their oversized paintings of *trains, ships, airplanes, donkeys, that carry their gifts* to distant friends

ROOM SETTINGS. These also may be simply yet effectively portrayed, as when:
A hospital room is devised by covering two or three low classroom tables with white sheets or spreads to represent beds and adding a QUIET sign to the wall.
A *"tokonoma,"* corner of beauty in a Japanese home, is formed from four simple items: a low wooden stool, a floral or bird print hung above it, a low bowl with graceful branches placed on top of it, a flat cushion placed in front of it.

SETTINGS AND PROPERTIES

BACKGROUND SETTINGS ARE IMPORTANT

Background scenery is important because:

- It can provide the viewers their first clue about the subject of the play.

- It can capture interest before a single word is spoken or a single movement made.

- It can transport players and viewers to far places:
    to Dr. Schweitzer's hospital in Lambaréné
    to a Navaho hogan
    to the home of Mary and Joseph in Nazareth

- It can give children opportunity to work with originality in its creation.

TYPES OF BACKGROUND SETTINGS

There are various types of simple background settings, capable of being used in a variety of ways to create atmosphere and capture interest.

A PAINTED WINDOW. With white curtains painted on each side and books painted on shelves beneath, the window suggests a living room.

With shelves painted on each side and cereal boxes and fruit cans painted on the shelves, the window indicates a grocery store.

With designs in color and a Gothic shape, the window makes the setting for a church.

With one pane missing and another cracked, the window suggests the temporary home of a migrant worker.

A WALL OR CURTAIN. A bare wall or unadorned draperies may suggest, depending on the play itself, such settings as:

A monk's cell where he copies the Bible manuscript

A hospital room where a life is being saved

An open space in the jungle forest where children meet for games

OUTDOOR SCENES. Children's paintings identify the outdoor scenes, as:

A fence identifies a yard or park.

Bright colored clothing drying on lines stretched from one tall tenement building to another identifies a crowded section of a city.

Rows of tomato vines become the fields where the migrant families work.

A ship's railing, a life preserver, blue sky in the distance show the setting to be a ship's deck.

Tall "stone" columns with nearby trees represent the courtyard of a palace.

A SCREEN. A three-panel screen is a most versatile property. When arranged to form a room of three closed sides, with the fourth open, it may become:

SETTINGS AND PROPERTIES

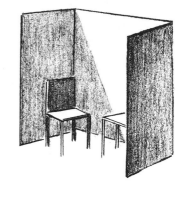

Dr. Carver's laboratory
A Hebrew Succoth booth
The nursery in a church neighborhood center
Joseph's room in the Egyptian palace

When the screen is straightened, it may be placed on the stage at any angle and with a painted illustration thumb-tacked to it become a property, as:

A fireplace
The manger
The altar of the high priest
The pump in Helen Keller's yard

CHILDREN MAY BECOME THE SCENERY

PRIMARY children delight in becoming the scenery and often themselves think of ways to contrive it, as in the following situations:

The idea of Stephen and his group surprised and pleased everyone. Stephen, following an attack of polio, came to class in a wheel chair, but this in no way limited his participation in group activities. The chair proved to be a real asset when the group played the story "The Good Samaritan."

"I'll sit in my chair and be some scenery along the road," Stephen announced.

The children liked the idea and pushed it further. "You be the rocks! We'll cover you with crumpled up paper and paint it to look rocky and dangerous."

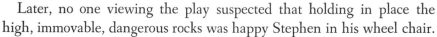

Later, no one viewing the play suspected that holding in place the high, immovable, dangerous rocks was happy Stephen in his wheel chair.

Betsey in her bright red dress became the Little Red Lighthouse. Holding a flashlight in her hands high over her head, she flashed its light first in one direction, then another, warning the boats that passed the sandy shore. Other children portrayed the boats that passed in rhythms: the canoes, ferryboats, coal barges, steamers.

First grade boys became a forest, each boy holding a real tree branch.

Girls became falling snowflakes as they turned and twirled in their white dresses, with balls of white cotton fluttering from streamers tied to their wrists.

Boys and girls became waves. With lengths of blue cheesecloth across their shoulders, they moved in rhythmic patterns to the center of the platform and out, bending low, then higher and higher as they moved against the background that showed ships—ships that sail the ocean bringing to America people like Michael Pupin and Jacob Riis from lands across the sea, bearing gifts to share.

PROPERTIES

Like settings, properties are not necessary. They can be imagined. When older children include them, they sometimes make them.

 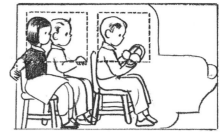

TREES

An upright coat rack can be transformed into any kind of needed tree. Take six large sheets of newspaper and paste them together, two at the top, two in the middle, two at the bottom, to make one large sheet, longer than the coat rack is high.

Outline and paint the tree on the paper, making the trunk about twice the width of the coat rack. Push the "arms" of the coat rack through holes cut in the leafy branches of the painted tree.

CHRISTMAS TREES are green, with painted on colored balls and other decorations and interestingly shaped packages tied with gay ribbons.

APPLE TREES are green with painted on red apples or real ones tied with green string to hang down from the poked through "arms" of the coat rack.

TRUCKS AND CARS

Realistic trucks and cars are achieved by painting the design on a length of paper about four by nine feet, then attaching it with staples or thumbtacks to a narrow but firm wooden frame about the same size. According to its painted on gadgets, the car may become a migrant family's truck, a missionary's station wagon, an evangelist's chapel car.

Windows cut into place enable the occupants seated in first grade chairs placed behind the car to look out and at the same time to hold the frame in upright position as though the car were traveling.

LARGE ANIMALS

Large animals often appear in favorite stories that are to be played, as: The three camels that carry the traditional Three Kings, who bring gifts to children in Puerto Rico and Spain in the Christmas season

The colt that is himself a gift in the Japanese carol "Birthday Presents" (from *The Whole World Singing*)

To create animals is worth the time and thought. Outline them in chalk on large wrapping paper or newspaper sheets pasted together. Paint as desired. Cut out and mount on a wooden frame as suggested above for trucks.

COSTUMES

Costumes also may be imagined. They are not necessary to the story play. KINDERGARTEN children do not need costumes in their plays.

PRIMARY children can "take them or leave them"; their story play will be enjoyed regardless.

Many JUNIORS prefer costumes and want them as complete and as authentic as possible. Costumes often make their play seem more real to them; they give added pleasure to the wearer and often help him to play his part with more conviction.

HEADDRESS
Of all possible costumes, the headdress probably is the most important:

- It immediately identifies the wearer—a jeweled crown for a king, a velvet turban for a Wise Man, a white starched cap for a nurse.
- It is simple to make.
- It is easy to put on and take off.

CLOTHING
Other simple items of clothing also may be easily achieved by combining ingenuity with a little work. "Good theater" demands brilliant rather than pastel colors for dresses, robes, capes, etc., and these articles are more effective if the hems and trimmings are cleverly painted on

rather than sewed. Many an illusion worked out by the children appears quite genuine for those who see the play.

A nondescript brown tunic becomes a *garment of splendor* when trimmed with a border scroll of scarlet and gilt put on by a child using paints imaginatively.

An ordinary black garment is transformed into a *royal robe* when trimmed with bands of "ermine," narrow strips of white cotton daubed with occasional blobs of black liquid shoe polish.

A plain laundry cardboard from a father's shirt, cut in intricate design, becomes a *priceless crown* when painted on rubies, emeralds, and sapphires are surrounded by pasted on glitter from the dime store.

PALESTINIAN CLOTHING

A twenty inch square of mother's discarded sheet becomes the bright *headdress* of the Palestinian shepherd, which the "shepherd" makes for himself by alternating white stripes with wide colored crayoned ones.

Striped awning or pillowcase material makes his *outer garment*.

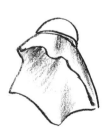

Cardboard shaped to his feet becomes the *sandals*, which are held in place with masking tape underneath and crisscrossed around his ankles.

A sawed off broom handle with cardboard crook thumbtacked in place at one end becomes his *staff*.

COSTUME HELP FROM PARENTS

NO. For mothers to meet at school, church, or someone's home, bringing portable sewing machines to turn out, assembly line fashion, twenty identical green grasshopper suits and fifteen identical yellow jonquil

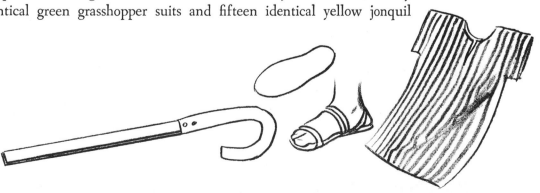

dresses does not help the children to develop their capacities, though it may give the parents a good time, satisfy their urge to help, and increase their pride in their children.

YES. Instead, mothers' most appreciated help is to provide needed materials so the children may make their own costumes: a yard of gray cheesecloth for the cocoon; a three yard length of pretty pink muslin for the Indian sari; father's worn but clean white shirt for the hospital patient's bedgown.

ADDITIONAL. Also parents may provide a supply of basic costume materials to become a welcome permanent possession of every school and church. Although part of the "learning" and fun for children in playing a story is to plan and create costumes for each play, materials such as the following may be reused creatively time after time, differently with each play:

Two dozen forty-eight inch lengths of good quality cheesecloth, assorted colors, including white, black, gray

Several yard lengths of drapery material, stripes and conventional designs rather than floral patterns

A dozen worn sheets freshly laundered, white and colored

A box of assorted artificial flowers, cloth and paper

A box of discarded costume jewelry, the bulky kind: bracelets, necklaces, large pins, earrings

MAKE-UP

Make-up as such has no place in children's story play. It throws the emphasis in the wrong place. No child should attempt to achieve the outward physical appearance of the character he is acting, by changing his skin color, for example. It is the character's inner feeling that he is striving to portray.

5

Pantomime and Tableaux

PANTOMIME

Pantomime is the simplest way for children to play a story. In it the characters move but do not speak. KINDERGARTEN AND YOUNGER PRIMARY CHILDREN enjoy this way because it gives them the freedom of "acting" and moving around without having to remember words. By moving eyes, mouth, facial muscles, legs, arms, body, they may portray the character's age or youth; his anger, surprise, fear, haste, clumsiness, weariness. Words are not needed.

For children to project a story without dialogue is as much a challenge to their ingenuity and skill as it is for their parents to act convincingly a difficult word in charades.

Pantomime is mostly for fun. KINDERGARTEN children play it for their own enjoyment. PRIMARY children sometimes share their pantomime story with others. When this technique for story play is used for an unfamiliar story, narration by the leader is necessary. When the children know the story well, the play may then unfold in the familiar sequence without a narrator, each action anticipated, then executed at the proper moment and in the proper manner, to the delight of all.

55

INTRODUCING THE PANTOMIME

Pantomime may be introduced with the closing words of the story, as:

"And so when Mr. New Year asked Mr. Old Year about the twelve children who would be coming to his house, what do you suppose Mr. Old Year told him about the first child, January? . . . Good! Show us the ice skating . . . Who will act another idea about January?"

Each child in the group may choose a month to act, or two children may plan together, in some such way as this:

March: trees bending in the wind

April: holding an umbrella and walking in the rain

May: arranging May baskets and hanging them on doorknobs

EXPANDING THE PANTOMIME

Individual pantomime expands readily into group pantomime. The teacher in retelling the above story adapts it to suit the moment. One child acts the part of Mr. Old Year, one the part of Mr. New Year, twelve others are the twelve months, as the story narration directs them:

"And so Mr. Old Year with all his children behind him walked the long, long distance to where Mr. New Year was waiting. 'Here they are,' he said, 'all twelve of them. I'll count them to be sure, one . . . two . . . three . . .'

"Mr. New Year looked happy. 'I like my new family.' Then he looked worried. 'But how can I tell one child from another?'

"Mr. Old Year laughed out loud. 'That's easy! They are not at all alike. I'll show you! . . . January, come here! Show Mr. New Year what you can do.' . . .

"Mr. New Year liked January so much he gave him a big hug.

"Then Mr. Old Year said, 'February, you're the shortest child. Show Mr. New Year what you can do.' . . .

"Mr. New Year liked February so well he patted him on the head. . . ." etc. etc.

PANTOMIME AND TABLEAUX

"And after Mr. New Year got acquainted with all the children he was so tired . . . he fell asleep . . . and the children did, too . . . and Mr. Old Year was so sad he went off home alone wiping away his tears with a great big handkerchief. . . ."

STORIES FOR PLAYING IN PANTOMIME

FOR KINDERGARTEN

"Children Around the World"

This picture book series, describing toys, games, pets, and homes of other lands, offers excellent material for pantomime by small children.

FOR PRIMARY

"The Mischief Maker," from *The Round Window*

FOR BOTH KINDERGARTEN AND PRIMARY

Rosita: a Little Girl of Puerto Rico (see page 160)

This story is given in detail below, as adapted for playing by children. The scenery and properties may be real or imagined. If real, Rosita's home may be represented on one side of the room or stage and the church with its crèche on the other side (see Settings: A Screen, page 48).

The *characters* played by the children are: Rosita and her parents, characters in the Nativity scene—the mother, father, shepherds, and Three Kings, also the Three Kings in Rosita's dream.

The *teacher-narrator* pauses at the appropriate places to permit time for the pantomimed action, which is indicated in the text below by italicized words. The slight changes from the story text are to insure smooth and continuous action.

57

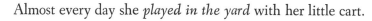

A STORY TO PANTOMIME
NARRATOR: Rosita lived in Puerto Rico.

Almost every day she *played in the yard* with her little cart.

One day while she *was playing*, Mamá *called to her* from the doorway, *"Come,* let me measure your new dress."

Rosita *turned this way and that way* while Mamá measured.

She *liked* her new dress.

Soon Papá from his place under the tree *called to Rosita,* *"Come,* see what I am making for you."

Rosita *jumped up and down* while she *watched* Papá *make a bowl* out of a gourd.

She *liked* her new bowl.

Rosita *took the bowl* to Mamá.

Mamá *filled it* with rice and beans.

Rosita *sat down* in the doorway and *ate* the good rice and beans.

One day Papá *called to Mamá and Rosita,* "It is Christmas. We will go to church."

Papá and Mamá *held Rosita's hands* while they *walked along* the path to the church.

At church they *saw* a Christmas scene: the mother, the father, the baby asleep in the manger, men with sheep, men with camels.

Mamá *said,* "The mother and father love their baby."

58

PANTOMIME AND TABLEAUX

Papá *said,* "The shepherds want to see the baby."

Mamá *said,* "The Three Kings bring him presents."

Rosita *ran to stand near* the shepherds.

She *ran to stand near* the Three Kings.

She *ran to stand near* the baby.

Papá, Mamá, and Rosita *walked home.*

Rosita *told them,* "I wish we had the baby. I wish I had a dolly."

But she had no dolly, so she *played* again with the little cart.

Mamá and Papá *sat* by the door.

Rosita *put a heavy stone* in the cart and *pulled* . . . and the cart broke.

Rosita *showed the broken cart* to Mamá.

Mamá *said,* "Never mind. Even a broken cart will hold grass for the Three Kings who ride through the world to-night. Their camels will be hungry."

Papá *brought grass,* and Rosita *put the grass* into the broken cart.

Rosita *said,* "The camels will be thirsty."

She *filled her bowl* with water.

That night Rosita *put her sleeping mat* beside the door.

That night Rosita *put her cart and bowl* beside her mat.

Then she *was soon asleep* on the mat.

Rosita dreamed that the Three Kings *came riding* to her home, *came riding* right to her mat.

In the dream one King *carried the grass* out to the camels.

They ate it all up.

One King *carried the water* out to the camels. They drank it all up.

One King *looked straight at Rosita* and *said*, "Thank you, little girl."

In the morning Rosita *woke up*.

She *looked beside the mat* for the grass and for the water.

What she *saw* made her *jump up* quickly from the mat.

She *picked up the bowl*. Inside was a dolly.

She *picked up the broken cart*. Inside was a new little cart.

Rosita *hugged her dolly*.

She *pulled her cart* to show Mamá and Papá.

"Presents," she *sang out*. "The Three Kings left me presents."

Mamá and Papá *hugged* Rosita.

They *liked* to see her happy.

TABLEAUX

A tableau is a living scene without motion and without sound. The actors neither move nor speak. Actions may be suggested by an extended arm, bowed head, turned body,

60

PANTOMIME AND TABLEAUX

raised foot, but the pose is held without movement for the brief moment it is viewed. The tableau sometimes is called "picture posing."

Its purpose for younger children

The purpose of a tableau for younger children is usually to illustrate some particular story incident or picture connected with the current study material, as a means for remembering it.

For this age a tableau also may be used as a game: one or two children planning the pose and executing it, the others guessing it. The composition of their pictures needs to be simple, and some movement is to be expected, because this age does not and should not keep motionless.

Its purpose for older children

For older children, a tableau is effective in worship, as when their posed Thanksgiving scene lifts hearts to a new feeling of thankfulness for food, family, life itself, or when their posed scene of "The Angelus" brings a new awareness of the meaning of worship in the lives of all people.

When juniors use the tableau in this way, they may devise draperies or a frame to enclose the grouping, add colorful costumes and special lighting, and work out appropriate recorded music.

Older groups also like to use tableaux to illustrate a favorite story and do so by placing a series of informal groups around the classroom, thereby including all members of the class in the activity. If the story is familiar the viewers need no explanation of the scenes; if unfamiliar, a narrator tells the story as the viewers move from scene to scene.

SUGGESTED SOURCES FOR TABLEAUX

Each tableau in the scenes described below may include one character or several, depending on the number of children in the class and their interest in the project. All properties and scenery are suggested by those appearing in the actual illustrations; providing them is the children's responsibility. Child or teacher becomes the narrator.

KINDERGARTEN

From the picture book *Children and Their Toys Around the World*

"Ahmed's Pipes" (Arabia)

(Properties—pipes painted on paper, then cut out)

"Shu Chin's Kite" (China)

(Properties—kites painted on paper, strings put into place, then kites attached high on a background curtain and strings held in children's hands as though kites are flying)

"Shanti and Prem Look for Toys" (India)

(Properties—toys painted on cardboard, then cut out to stand upright)

The narrator introduces the series simply: "Our posed pictures show toys that are enjoyed in different lands. Here is Ahmed from Arabia with his musical pipes. . . . This is Shu Chin with his friends. You can tell their favorite game is flying kites. . . ." etc.

PRIMARY

From the picture book *Children at Worship Around the World*

"A Place of Beauty" (Japan)

(Setting—low table, bowl of flowers, a picture of the Nativity)

"Thanks for Food" (Philippine Islands)

(Setting—low table, low stools, bowls of food)

PANTOMIME AND TABLEAUX

"Gifts for the World's Children" (U.S.A.)
(Setting—table, world globe)

"Bedtime Prayer" (Chile)
(Setting—chair, doll, bed)

The narrator may say, "All around the world people worship God in the same ways that we know. . . . Here Yasuko makes her home beautiful. . . . Here Matio and his family bow their heads while Father offers thanks for the good harvest of rice. . . ." etc.

JUNIOR

From the picture album *World Friends: Spreading the Gospel*
"The Teacher Points to the Words" (India)
(Setting—blackboard, pointing stick, the Holy Bible)

"What Does the Picture Say?" (Thailand)
(Setting—chairs and lesson pictures)

"I Will Sing to the Lord" (Puerto Rico)
(Setting—tambourine, dried gourds)

"A Church on Wheels" (U.S.A.)
(Setting—a worship center, chairs, the Holy Bible)

The narrator begins, "If Christian teachings are to reach around the world to people who do not know them, the Bible that contains these teachings must be printed in many languages so that all may understand as they read or listen. This teacher in India is helping her class to know the Bible. . . . Here a teacher uses pictures to teach. . . . Here children sing the story in song. . . ." etc.

6

Rhythms and Music

RHYTHMS

The art of rhythms is sometimes described as the art of group movement. This is true, but there is more than this, for the movement, if effective, results from an "inner feeling," a feeling so real and compelling that the person finds himself being caught up in the mood of the particular situation being portrayed and reacting to it in a natural, convincing, and true to life manner.

As a form of story play, children of all ages may participate in rhythms, but its real worth for each player is measured by the degree to which he is able to catch the mood of the situation and match his movements to it—whether the mood be one of gaiety, like that felt by a child who visits the circus and becomes what he sees: the marching leader of the band, the tumbling clown on the seesaw, the galloping horse in the race; or one of determination, like that felt by the explorers as they pushed and pulled, pushed and pulled, to loosen and move the rock embedded deep in the wagon trail; or one of wonder, surprise, and perhaps fear, like that felt by the shepherds one long ago night on the Bethlehem hills.

64

RHYTHMS AND MUSIC

VALUES OF RHYTHMS

Rhythms are used as *a means of expression that aids in the growth and development of children.* Younger children, always exuberant and on the move, play rhythmically all the experiences of their family's day. They roll out cookies, make beds, rake leaves in the yard, sweep the garage floor, with all the feeling of a mother or daddy. And when this spontaneous play is not discouraged nor frowned upon by parents or teachers, the children continue to express themselves freely and creatively and joyously.

If the child is curbed too much in his younger years, his natural freedom of expression seems to be gone by the time he reaches fifth or sixth grade. Shy and self-conscious, he may refuse altogether to join in rhythmic story play.

At such times the teacher helps him by permitting no mention of shortcomings and by never urging participation unduly. Eventually children themselves solve the problem by catching the spirit and mood of the players and deciding for themselves that they want to be included. When children participate in rhythms by their own choice, the shy one often loses his self-consciousness, the show-off less frequently bids for attention, the bossy one begins to comply with the group's ideas, the overactive one tends to slow down, the aggressive one learns to take his turn.

A group may even suggest trying to interpret increasingly difficult moods rather than continuing to do the simple ones with which they are already familiar.

Rhythms provide *a natural way to bring the largest number of children into the play.*

Whatever the size of the group, everyone may be included in rhythmic play. There may be four squirrels or ten hiding nuts in secret places, one weather vane or six turning to signal that storms are on the way, eight hungry people or eighteen moving in their search for food.

65

Rhythms serve as a means of *bringing a different and unusual touch to a story that is "acted" in the regular way.*

In almost every story there is at least one incident or mood that may be portrayed in rhythms. Children and teacher only need to examine the story in order to find it. With or without music, such a movement brings a freshness, newness, and charm unlike that of the spoken word.

A *second grade,* in playing the story of Helen Keller's childhood, ingeniously used a train rhythm to show the passage of time and distance when Helen's teacher-to-be, Anne Sullivan, traveled by train from her school in Massachusetts to Helen's home in Alabama. The entire class became the long line of cars, each car held to the other by each pair of arms being locked around the waist of the child in front. The train choo-chooed rhythmically in and out, across and around the stage, coming to a jolting halt on the "engineer's" called out signal, "All out for Baltimore," "All out for Nashville," then starting again at the pull of the pretend whistle and the call, "All aboard."

A *fifth grade* used rhythms to picture a game enjoyed centuries ago by a young prince of India. Associates of the young prince visited him daily, and together the boys stood straight and tall beside the courtyard wall. From the pretend quiver strapped across his shoulders, each boy moved

in unison with the others to remove his arrow, place it in position in the bow, pull the bowstring taut, then send the arrow straight to its target.

Again and again these movements were repeated, a colorful rhythmic pattern that contributed the unusual and unexpected.

Rhythms are a means of *catching the mood and feelings of the story characters.*

When this happens the movements seem genuine and real, not mechanically directed by the leader. Children *feel:*

- The *weariness* of the migrant worker as he walks slowly to the field

- His *tiredness* as he bends to pick the berries from the vines and place them in the baskets

- His *exhaustion* as he moves along the row to begin the monotonous routine again

Each player interprets the feelings in his own way, a hand pushing back rumpled hair from a forehead, a hand wiping away perspiration, a brief rest on bended knee, a hand reaching to ease back and leg muscles that are tense and rigid. . . .

For the period of the play the player is the migrant worker, speaking no word, but telling the story vividly through action.

THE TEACHER'S PART

TO BE ADVENTUROUS

The teacher with an adventurous spirit who is willing to try the un-tried will in time no longer be afraid of or ignore rhythms as a way of playing a story. He will welcome this kind of story play as a valuable teaching tool with which he can deepen for the children the meaning of the story itself and provide an outlet for their imaginations.

TO BE IMAGINATIVE

Always the teacher uses his own imagination, as he searches for mean-ingful ways to use rhythmic play. With practice he trains himself to find possibilities in simple and obvious, yet usually by-passed, places.

TO ENCOURAGE THE CHILDREN

As narrator, the teacher first tells the story to be played. He draws from the children ideas about the story situations that can be interpreted with movements and what those movements will be. The story may be told one day, reviewed and rhythms planned the next, reviewed and inter-preted the third day.

Sometimes the children themselves initiate the rhythmic play with ideas that are appropriate to the weather, season, or story. Such impromptu suggestions usually are carried out immediately.

TO KEEP THE PLAY PURPOSEFUL

The teacher's manner, plus a general atmosphere of purposeful, serious activity within the classroom, do much to assure the children's continuous interest. Also, when the activity is adequately planned by the children and the expected responses understood by them, there is less likelihood of disorder or inattention.

68

RHYTHMS AND MUSIC

At no time is the play permitted to become aimless or uncontrolled. At the first sign of restlessness or of the group getting out of hand, the teacher immediately lowers his voice and directs the tempo of the activity to a slower and quieter one, as, "Suddenly . . . all was still. . . . Everyone come on tiptoe . . . slow -ly . . . slow -ly . . . to form a circle in the grass by the big tree, here."

TO MEET THE PROBLEM OF MUSICAL ACCOMPANIMENT

When the teacher is also a pianist, he often will use musical directions for the story play, improvising as the situation demands. If he does not play the piano, his voice, clap of hands, a drum beat, or musical recordings can be effectively used in place of music. Any one of these is usually better than a poor accompanist.

When there is an able accompanist, the teacher plans and works closely with him prior to each session. The accompanist then needs no verbal directions during the play, other than those given to the children. He has the appropriate music either at his fingertips or readily accessible in the books in front of him. There are times when the accompanist personally catches the value and significance of this imaginative kind of story play and becomes so excited about it that he willingly searches until he finds just the right music to express the particular mood or movement, or carefully works out his own improvisations until they express it to his satisfaction.

The accompanist's role is an important one, and it can become as highly skilled, as versatile, and as valuable as he cares to make it.

SUGGESTED SOURCES FOR MUSICAL ACCOMPANIMENT

Children's hymnals often include instrumental music of varied tempi that are appropriate for rhythmic accompaniment. Such music is contained in the songbooks *Sing, Children, Sing; Songs for Little Children; Hymns for Primary Worship; Hymns for Junior Worship* (see page 158).

THE CHILDREN'S PART

KINDERGARTEN AND FIRST GRADE CHILDREN use rhythms for their own pleasure, each child catching the mood and executing the action in his own way and with no thought of repeating it except for themselves, because the first playing brought pleasure and satisfaction.

At such times the entire group moves together, or a few within the group carry on the movement while the others watch. In both situations each child feels for himself and acts for himself, whether sorry, lonely, or mad, whether jumping, skating, or hammering.

Possible responses may be previously discussed with the children, but there is no attempt to keep each person's movement within a pattern.

OLDER PRIMARIES AND JUNIORS are able to express both serious and light moods, and each child does it in his own way. They also like to interpret some kinds of action in a definite group pattern, as when small groups move together within a larger group, each small group executing its own movement, yet all fitting together to present the whole picture, as when portraying a playground scene.

Three such small groups are described below, but others could be included, playing tennis, rolling a hoop, etc.

A SUGGESTED RHYTHM PLAY—A Playground Scene

Two children pretend to turn a rope, the third child jumping it. In the same tempo two others pretend to play ball, one throwing the ball, the other catching it, then returning it for the first child to catch. Two others pretend to seesaw, one rising on tiptoe as the other takes a stooping position, then reversing the movements, up-down, up-down.

The tempo in this rhythm is one-two, each group doing its own action to this beat. Jumping rope: *one* (arm up to turn rope), *two* (arm down to complete the turn), *one* (child ready to jump), *two* (child jumps). Playing ball: *one* (child throws ball), *two* (child catches ball), *one* (ball is

returned), *two* (ball is caught). Seesaw: *one* (child stands high and his partner stoops), *two* (standing child stoops, and stooping child stands).

When each small group thinks only of itself and each person moves simultaneously with his partner, the beat is not difficult to keep. The several co-ordinated group movements make a graceful, smooth, flowing pattern that often expresses the scene's idea more realistically than words.

STORIES IN WHICH RHYTHMS MAY BE INCLUDED

WHEN THE ENTIRE STORY IS PLAYED IN RHYTHMS

Manuel: a Little Boy of Mexico (kindergarten and first grade)

As here presented, the narration is adapted from the original story by Jeanette Perkins Brown (see page 160) and may be played with or without music. The teacher may tell the story one day and have the children review, plan, and play it the following day. Movements are sufficiently varied to permit each child a choice of action. Of course, some of the children will want to act out the various amusements in the park!

The story is easily shortened by the omission of one or more of the park sequences. In the acting, a pause comes after each action while the children listen for the next part of the story. As the story progresses and the children's interest mounts, they will enter the play without further invitation to do so.

If there is musical accompaniment, the pianist of course is familiar with the plan of the story and with his music, so that he can move readily from one story situation to another.

NARRATOR: Manuel and his small brother Pepito were very happy. The next day was a *fiesta* day in their country of Mexico, and on this holiday they were going with their mother and father for a picnic in the park.

Who can show us how happy they were?

(*A few will respond by skipping, hopping, clapping hands, twirling. Pause . . . then the story continues.*)

NARRATOR: That night the two boys couldn't go to sleep for a long time. They thought only of the picnic day.

Who can show us how they curled up in bed and tried to sleep?

(*Others will volunteer. Pause . . . then the story continues.*)

NARRATOR: Alas! Next morning when they awakened, Pepito was sick. He could not go to the park. Mother must stay at home with him. Manuel was most unhappy until Papá whispered a secret to him.

Who will whisper it?

(*By this time there will be no further need of suggestions. The children who want to respond will do so as the story directs. And they will know that they must expect the pause before the story continues.*)

NARRATOR: Soon Papá and Manuel said good-by and went to the park. There were so many sights to see! Men riding galloping horses! (*Action. Pause.*)

Monkeys hanging from tree branches! (*Action. Pause.*)

Families eating their good picnic lunches! (*Action. Pause.*)

Little dogs jumping through their hoops! (*Action. Pause.*)

Boys and girls riding in red airplanes on the merry-go-round! (*Action. Pause.*)

Boys and girls holding tight to their bright balloons so the wind would not blow them away! (*Action. Pause.*)

NARRATOR: When they got home, Papá and Manuel found that Pepito was much better. Pepito and Mamá were glad to see Manuel and Papá. They said, "Tell us what you saw at the park." So Manuel and Papá told everything they could remember.

Which ones do you remember? (*Action. Pause.*)

"Why, you've brought us the park," Mamá and Pepito said. "That was our secret," said Manuel and Papá. Everyone laughed and was happy. (*Action.*)

WHEN AN ENTIRE SCENE IS PLAYED IN RHYTHMS

"A Chance for School," from *The Round Window* (Primary)
The entire play included:
  Scene I: At home in the city • *Scene II:* On the train going to the new home in the country • *Scene III:* A second home in the city • *Scene IV:* The playground up forty steps (see page 70) • *Scene V:* In Cece's school

WHEN PART OF A SCENE IS PLAYED IN RHYTHMS

"White Sails and Blue Sea," from *Stories of the Book of Books* (Junior)
Scene I: On deck of the sailboat *Surat*, 1874. Conversation among the passengers as in the story.
  Rhythms: Sailors moving in unison as together they untie each rope in turn, swing it, and toss it back to the dock.

Scene II: Inside the ship's cabins. Conversation as in the story.

Rhythms: Sailors bringing in the heavy chest filled with New Testaments, resting, pulling, resting, pulling.

Scene III: The ship at sea.

(A ship is painted on paper and hung at the back of the stage.)

Narrator relates the incidents from the story of the long, tiresome trip and the passengers' fears that they may never reach shore.

Rhythms: Four groups of children express in unison the changing action of the ocean waters as they move against the ship.

One group, wearing gray scarves, interpret the quiet sea waters against the ship.

Another, in blue and green scarves, become the waters of a clear, sunny day that play gently against the ship.

A third, in yellow, create the feeling of the intense tropical heat beating down on sea and ship.

A fourth, in brown, purple, black, with strong, violent, swinging motions, portray the mighty storm.

Scene IV: A church pulpit nearly seventy-five years later. An old man, the son of one of the children from the wrecked *Surat,* follows the conversation in the story.

Rhythms: A children's choir with arms extended in an upward movement sing their praise and thanksgiving that the most important object on the *Surat* had been saved: "Rejoice, rejoice, rejoice, give thanks, and sing."

MUSIC

Children's response to music is usually one of natural interest. Certainly music has a unique power to help them grow in their understanding of others, for it speaks a universal language and transcends the barriers of age, background, and race.

74

RHYTHMS AND MUSIC

IT APPEALS IN MANY WAYS

Children of all ages love to *listen* to music—as it is sung or played on an instrument or on a record.

They love to *sing* for themselves songs that relate to things they are doing, to places they have visited or studied about, to the life of boys and girls in other lands.

Many times music becomes part of children's *informal dramatics,* particularly as it centers about favorite holidays or around an interesting unit of study.

SOURCES OF THE STORY SONG

Many songs tell a story! A mother's lullaby, a festival celebration, customs of another land, a workman at his work—these story ideas and many others are waiting to be lifted from the songbook and played by the children in their classroom.

When the teacher with questing eye begins to examine these many songs found between the covers of a book and to ask of each one, "Can the children play this in a story?" he is likely to discover a source of truly valuable story play material.

The song's own words may provide the play's dialogue. They give the directions for using it, whether it will be sung by an individual or by the group. They give certain clues for action, scenery, or properties. They provide for the use of imagination.

DRAMATIZING THE STORY SONG

In acting a story song, children discover that they have all the enjoyment of acting a regular story, plus the added fun of singing words instead of saying them. They also discover that singing a story in their own group or with several groups lifts spirits and joins hearts in a special way and brings the magic of friendliness and good will to the whole group.

In the classroom, acting the song will be for the group's own enjoyment. When several of the individual story songs are on the same theme they may be put together, each to become a scene or episode in a departmental service of worship, as described below.

PRIMARY

Early in the Christmas season, each of seven primary classes chose to dramatize a carol from another country. Using simple scenery and costumes and properties made by themselves, each class played its particular carol again and again in its own room and for its own enjoyment.

When the primary supervisor suggested that the seven scenes put together would tell the Christmas story in a new and unusual way, the children were pleased. "It can be our Christmas service of worship," they said.

In the course of further planning the question arose as to the song play's effectiveness for worship if the children tried to sing and act at the same time. The children said, "Each class knows all the carols. Let each class act its own song while the others sing it with them." To this excellent idea was added another—a group of ten parents were given copies of the songs in advance and invited to share in the service, sitting together near the piano, acting as a sort of adult choir to carry the story of each song in words, in case the children's voices did not "come through."

A third grade's painted scene of the Bethlehem hills at night, with the village seen in the distance, formed the background. Their stable scene was tacked to a screen and placed diagonally in center of stage left (see Background Settings: A Screen, page 48). In front of it were Mary and Joseph with the manger and its baby, the family forming a beautiful picture pose for the entire service.

All action in the story songs took place at stage right, moving to include the family group whenever the song words so directed.

The service was introduced briefly by the leader who, in simple phrases from the several favorite story songs, told the always new, yet always familiar story. Without further words, the wonderful story began to unfold as each class moved up to the low platform in sequence to play their part of it.

"O Little Town of Bethlehem" (*Hymns for Junior Worship*) was sung softly by a third grade.

"Wind Through the Olive Trees" was interpreted in rhythms by a first grade. Verse 1: a few children with green and gray scarves over their shoulders pretended to be the wind as it blew through the trees on the hill. Verse 2: others with white scarves became the sheep, some lying still, others scampering over the hillsides. Verse 3 was omitted. Verse 4: others, as children, went gaily to see the baby in the manger.

"A Christmas Antiphon," a song from Africa (*The Whole World Singing*), was sung by a second grade as they stood near the family, one child acting as leader, the others as the chorus. Two stanzas of their own creation were added and the movements enacted as the words directed:

"Shepherds saw the light and hurried. . . ."

"Wise men came and brought him presents. . . ."

"Lullaby to the Christ Child," an Armenian carol (*The Whole World Singing*), was sung by Mary, the mother, as she took the baby from the manger and held him in her arms.

"To Bethlehem, Come Let Us Go," a song from India (*The Singing Secret*), was played by a second grade, who, in Palestinian clothing and carrying crooks, became the shepherds. Advancing slowly from the rear of the room in three groups of four children each, the first group motioned to the second group, calling, "To Bethlehem, come let us go, praise, O praise, O praise!" The two groups sang the first stanza as they moved toward the platform. The second group then turned and called to the third group, "To Bethlehem, etc.," who joined them to move forward as they sang the second stanza. All shepherds knelt at the manger for the final verse, then moved quietly away.

"Bring a Torch, Jeannette, Isabella!", a French carol, was acted by a third grade. From various parts of the room, the children, as villagers with peasant type scarves over head and shoulders and carrying painted torches, called to one another, "Bring your torch, Jeannette," "Bring your torch, Isabella," and hurried to where the baby lay to "see how rosy his cheeks, how softly he sleeps."

"Birthday Presents" (*The Whole World Singing*): A first grade, as children from Japan, came to the manger and placed their gifts beside the baby—a cup of warm milk, an egg from the hen, a woolly shawl from the sheep.

"Carol from India" (*Roads to Christmas*): A third grade, as children from India, brought their gifts and placed them beside the manger—pomegranates, guavas, tinkling anklets, red turned up shoes, garlands of flowers.

"Mighty Day," a dramatic Negro spiritual (*The Whole World Singing*), was sung with praise and honor by all the

classes as they stood together for this closing part of their worship.

JUNIOR

A similar service, "Friends Around the World," is readily adaptable for juniors.

Boys and girls in each group will "become" persons of other lands as they learn the songs from that country and will create the appropriate scenery, properties, and costumes, if these are to be used. If a song seems "young" for the age group playing it, the leader recognizes this and explains that in story play juniors may impersonate any age; the ability to do this with reality is a sign the "actors" are feeling and thinking as do the "younger" characters they represent. The service may be developed from the following songs found in *The Whole World Singing* or from similar ones in other volumes.

"Friendship Song" may introduce the theme, a child from each of the play countries coming in turn to the group of singers to "hold out his friendly hands the circle to complete."

From Hawaii: "With Needle and Thread"
The children with real needles and thread sing as they work and pretend to sew the pretty flower chains that they have already made in class sessions. They may then go out among the other children and put the chains around their necks.

From China: "Yangtze Boatmen's Chantey"
The children, wearing wide brimmed flat hats made from large sheets of heavy paper, sing in rhythm as they pole their boats against the stream.

From the Congo: "The Magic Tom-Tom"
Half the class may sing the words as the others do the action. Their scenery may be a tree painted as background, monkeys and birds painted on cardboard, cut out, and hung in the tree, and drums fashioned from family size cereal boxes.

From India: "Balloon Song"
Boys may sing two verses and girls two, as they carry out whatever action seems appropriate.

From Japan: "My Doll"
One member of the class, in kimono, may be chosen for this part, acting the story in pantomime as the others in the class sing it.

From East Africa: "Seeds We Bring"
The properties of this song can be effectively imagined since the actions are specific.

"Round the World" provides an appropriate closing when sung as a prayer by all the groups.

80

7

Plays in a Box

MOVING PICTURES

The "moving picture" is a series of story illustrations painted or crayoned on sheets of the same size paper, pasted side by side in proper sequence, then pulled past an opening in a box and thus viewed as a movie.

This form of story play is suitable for PRIMARIES and JUNIORS and becomes as simple or elaborate as the children's whims, abilities, and imaginations and the materials available permit.

PURPOSE

The purpose of the moving picture is not to introduce a new and interesting craft activity, but to present another form of creative story play, by means of which children may assume the characters of the pictured people, speak their lines, and dramatize their gestures.

HOW TO PREPARE

The movie box may be almost any kind, from a grocer's carton, plain and undecorated, to a made-for-the-purpose wooden box with gaily painted curlicues of gilt, a border of

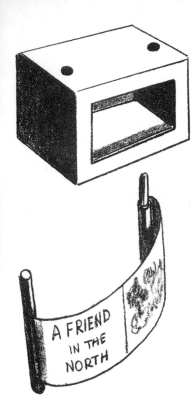

crimson, and a decorated cloth curtain to pull across the "stage" opening at the beginning and end of the performance, in true theater style.

To make the theater, cut an opening in the front of the box to allow a two or three inch frame around the opening. Cut two lengths of broom handle or inch wide dowel stick to be four to five inches longer than the box is high. Cut two holes in the top and bottom of the box, one near each end, and fit the rollers inside.

Paste together, side by side, the series of story illustrations. Attach the left side of the first picture to the left-hand roller, and the right side of the final picture to the right-hand roller. Wind up so that all are on the right-hand roller. As the story unfolds, the pictures turn from right to left and rewind on the left-hand roller.

The children's part

Children, of course, make the theater and the pictured illustrations and portray the characters, speaking the appropriate dialogue as each illustration comes into view in the frame.

A child also may act as announcer to give such information as:

* The general area of the class study

* The title of the story play and why this particular story was chosen

* The characters in the play

* The group's wish that the viewers will like and understand its message

82

PLAYS IN A BOX

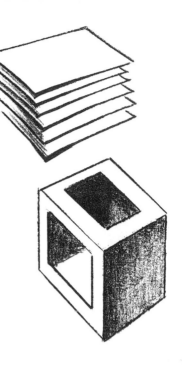

Stories to use

Any story or class experience may be presented in moving pictures: stories with animal characters—elephants, rabbits, donkeys—are especially effective to portray this way, for they may be seen in the pictures and heard as interpreted by the children's voices.

FOR FIRST GRADE
Nezbah's Lamb
Keiko's Birthday

FOR SECOND AND THIRD GRADE
"God's Gift to Paquito," from *The Singing Secret*
"The Boy in the Truck," from *The Missionary Story Hour*
"The Secret Cup," from *The Missionary Story Hour*

FOR JUNIORS
"Friend in the North," from *Bright Pathways*
"The Old Story in a New Land," from *We Gather Together*
"The Gift of a Song," from *The Missionary Story Hour*

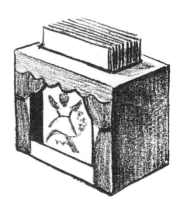

THE "KAMISHIBAI"

The *kamishibai* (kah-mee-shee-bye), a paper theater in a box, is a Japanese version of "moving pictures." It is a story-telling device that can be used in any country. In Japan, the story man with his *kamishibai* mounted on the rear of his bicycle rides along until he comes to a group of children. Leaving his bicycle, he walks among the children, gaining their attention by clapping together two wooden blocks, ringing a small bell, or sounding notes on a flute.

The Japanese children, anticipating the story, happily follow the story man and take their places in front of his paper theater. With a flourish, the story man opens the *kamishibai,* which becomes the stage, and fits into place a whole set of bright picture cards. On the first one is printed the story's title, on all the others are painted the story's brightly colored illustrations. The words of the story appear on the backs of the pictures so that they can be read aloud. The story that accompanies a picture appears on the back of the preceding picture.

When the children are quiet, the story man begins to tell his story and with changing voice and appropriate gestures continues to the climax, when he stops, stretches out his hand, and waits to receive coins from the listeners. Then, satisfied with his payment, he completes his story.

How to prepare

The theater box, like the one used for moving pictures, may be of almost any variety; it needs the same kind of framed opening across the front and also across the back. In addition, there is a long, narrow slit cut across the top of the box.

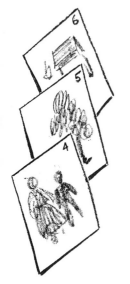

The pictured illustrations, like those of the moving picture, are made on identical size paper and are viewed through the box's framed opening, each in order as the story unfolds. Unlike the moving picture, they are not pasted side by side and attached to turning rollers, but each picture remains separate, and the complete set, arranged in sequence, is slipped down into the box through the narrow slit at the top.

As each picture is viewed, it is lifted from its place by the story man and replaced at the back of the set so that at the completion of the story the pictures are again in order for the next telling.

PLAYS IN A BOX

WHEN CHILDREN PLAY THE STORY

One child may become the story man and walk among the class, calling them to attention in Japanese fashion with the clap-clap-clap-clap of his wooden blocks. Then, taking his place beside the *kamishibai* paper theater, he shows each picture in turn while other children enact the story's scenes through dialogue and gesture.

SUGGESTED STORIES

Those that describe a *kamishibai:*

"Sadao and the Story Man," from *The Singing Secret* (P)

"Story Girl," from *Sidewalk Kids* (J)

Suggested ones to tell with a *kamishibai:*

"The 'Borrowed' Camp," from *The Boy with the Busy Walk* (P)

"Two Bright Eyes," from *The Round Window* (P)

"A Miner Strikes Pay Dirt," from *Stories of the Book of Books* (J)

"Visit from a Cobra," from *Chand of India* (J)

8

Play Actors of Paper and Cloth

PUPPET PLAYS

This kind of story play is suitable for PRIMARY and JUNIOR children.

A puppet is an artificial figure—man, child, giraffe, turtle—whose actions and dialogue are prompted and controlled by a person. They are fun to make, fun to use, and fun to watch. And there are many kinds. Some of the simplest ones are described below. More elaborate ones may be made, if the time to prepare them is available (see *Here's How and When*, Chapter 3).

KINDS OF PUPPETS

PUPPETS-ON-A-STICK are figures drawn on cardboard, decorated or "dressed" with crayons or paint, cut out, and glued or thumbtacked to a stick that is eight to ten inches in length (a ruler, dowel stick, or a plain stick picked up in the yard).

The puppet operator holds the stick as he sits on the floor behind his "stage," which may be a desk, table, or the back of a couch. He carefully conceals both the stick and his hand as he reaches up to maneuver the puppet character into its position on the stage.

PLAY ACTORS OF PAPER AND CLOTH

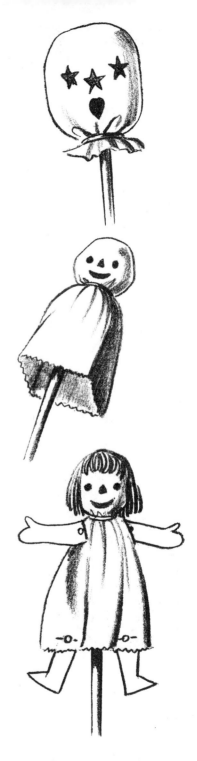

PAPER BAG PUPPETS are what their name implies, puppets created from paper bags.

Sometimes the bag becomes the head of the puppet. To make a *head puppet*, stuff and fill a Number 6 or 7 paper bag with crumpled newspaper. Push a twelve to fifteen inch stick inside, leaving half of it exposed to become the handle. Tie the open end of the bag securely. With paint or pasted on colored paper add facial features, bangs, braids, hat, collar, necklace, etc.

Operate the puppet like puppets-on-a-stick, the entire paper bag head of the figure showing as it appears above the stage.

Sometimes the bag becomes the head and body. To make a *head and body puppet,* tie some crumpled paper into the bottom of the paper bag to become the puppet's head, then invert the bag. The remainder of the bag becomes the body, to be decorated with painted clothing. *Arms* are added by stapling or tying at the figure's neck a six to eight inch length of folded paper. Or the operator's thumb and middle finger may become the arms, by extending them through holes cut on each side of the paper bag. *Hands* and *feet* cut from paper, felt, cardboard, or cloth may be glued or stapled into place.

HAND PUPPETS are another simple kind of puppet. They can be fashioned quite easily from a rubber ball and a piece of cloth.

To make the head, cut a one inch hole in the rubber ball and into it fit a rolled up piece of cardboard two to three inches long, to become the puppet's neck.

87

To make the dress, cut a piece of material about sixteen to eighteen inches long by ten to twelve inches wide, seam it on the side, gather it at the top, and sew this part to the cardboard collar to hang down as a loose garment.

To work the puppet, the operator's hand slips up underneath the dress and his index finger fits into the collar and directs the puppet's head movements. If there are sleeves or armhole openings in the dress, his thumb and middle finger go into these and become the puppet's arms. The arms move in all directions, pick up objects, hold them, or throw them.

Using puppets

Some leaders suggest that children first construct their puppets, then get to know them and what they can do and improvise conversations with them, before attempting to use them in real story play. Then, thoroughly acquainted with their puppets, the boys and girls are ready to plan their use in a special way.

With puppets becoming the characters and children speaking for them, any story or classroom experience may be played.

Values of puppet play for children

Puppets offer a wide scope for emotional expression

* The aggressive or domineering child, speaking through his puppet, may be able to release some of his own hostility.

* The shy and withdrawn child, speaking through his puppet, may develop friendliness and companionship with others.

Puppets provide many areas of learning

* Constructing a puppet requires skill: it takes careful and thoughtful use of materials and tools to combine them into figures that seem real, with personalities of their own.

88

PLAY ACTORS OF PAPER AND CLOTH

- Dressing a puppet requires imagination. It takes time, plus patience and creative ideas, to use paints and crayons to transform cloth into clothing for the figure, making it at the creator's wish a boy from Egypt, a girl from Mexico, a child from Holland.

- Operating a puppet requires control. It takes nimble fingers and concentration of mind to direct the puppet figure's movements so that it may dance, walk slowly, or fly through the air.

PUPPET PLAY TEACHES CHILDREN THE VALUE OF CO-OPERATION

- His puppet must take turns.

- His puppet rather than himself is the important one.

STORIES FOR PLAYING WITH PUPPETS

FOR PRIMARIES
"Market Day," from *Second Son*
"From Nobody to Somebody," from *The Missionary Story Hour*

FOR JUNIORS
"The Calico Cat," from *Blueberry Acres*
"One World for Johnny," from *Sidewalk Kids*

SHADOW PLAYS

Shadow plays are those performed by actors whose figures are viewed as shadows and silhouettes behind a sheet or screen, which may be attached across the front of a stage or a classroom doorway. The actors take their positions close to the sheet but not touching it. A bright light behind them shines against the sheet, making the shadow.

WHO PLAYS THEM

This kind of story play is suitable for JUNIORS.

THE KINDS OF STORIES TO BE PLAYED

Almost any story incident may be played in this manner. Comic and for-fun stories and incidents are especially appropriate, although thoughtful and serious subjects can be presented with impressive results. (See description of the Nativity story, page 92.)

WHEN CHILDREN BECOME THE SHADOW CHARACTERS

The light will need to be tried in various positions in order to find the right place for it, so as to get the best results.

The actor needs to try out various positions on the stage in order to achieve reality. He must stand sideways in profile against the sheet or his

PLAY ACTORS OF PAPER AND CLOTH

figure will appear as a "blob" without nose, ears, or mouth.

The actor needs to practice his movements. These must be slower and more exaggerated than in regular story play, if they are to be effective.

Properties, such as bowls, broom, sword, crown, may be fashioned from cardboard, since they are viewed only in the flatness of the shadow's one dimension.

Furniture properties, such as chairs, tables, etc., need to be placed in profile close to the screen.

WHEN CUTOUT FIGURES MAKE THE CHARACTERS

When cutout figures are used to play the story in shadow effect, the *stage* is a box, with its back and front cut away. The *curtain* is a piece of white cloth covering the open front of the box. The *light* is an electric bulb or very bright flashlight placed behind the box. The *story figures* are cut from poster cardboard and placed between the cloth and light to be viewed in silhouette against the "curtain." Their size, of course, is in proportion to the size of the curtain. Three or four figures outlined, then cut from one and the same strip of cardboard, are easier to manipulate at the same time than several single figures. When this cardboard strip is cut a little longer than the length of the front of the stage, it curves a bit when the ends are placed in position against the two front corners of the box, and thereby holds itself in position.

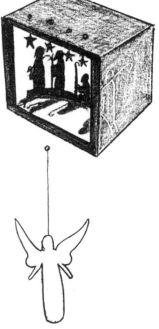

After each figure group is put in place at the front of the box, the light is turned on, and the children speak the lines for that scene. The light is then turned off briefly to permit the next figure group to be put in place. The narration then continues, and the process is repeated.

Using a shadow play

A sixth grade's Nativity story, described below, was planned to be shared with parents. The lines spoken by members of the class included the selection from the Gospel of Luke, Chapter 2, verses 8-20.

Scene I: On the hills near Bethlehem

Outlined figures of the *shepherds* appeared in profile and were cut from the same strip of cardboard.

Each of the six or seven *stars* was cut a different size, one larger than any of the others. They were suspended from the top of the box, high enough so the strings were concealed from the viewers' side.

At the time indicated in the narration an *angel,* also cut from cardboard, was suspended in the same way at the side of the scene.

FIRST CHILD: And in that region there were shepherds out in the field, keeping watch over their flock by night. Verses 8, 9.

SECOND CHILD (angel): Be not afraid . . . etc. Verses 10, 11, 12.

FIRST CHILD: Verse 13.

THE WHOLE CLASS: Verse 14.

FIRST CHILD: Verse 15a.

FIRST SHEPHERD: Let us go over to Bethlehem.

SECOND SHEPHERD: Let us see this thing that has happened.

THIRD SHEPHERD: Yes, let us go and see that which the Lord has made known to us.

(Lights out)

Scene II: In the stable

Figures of Mary, Joseph, the baby in the manger, a sheep and oxen in profile, cut from one strip of poster cardboard.

FIRST CHILD: Verse 16. (Pause)

(*Lights out*)

Scene III: In the stable
   Figures of shepherds in profile looking down at the baby, other figures at side, all cut from same strip of cardboard.

FIRST CHILD: Verse 17.

FIRST SHEPHERD: We were on the hillside watching over our sheep as usual.

SECOND SHEPHERD: Suddenly an angel appeared in the skies above.

THIRD SHEPHERD: The glory of the Lord shone round about.

FIRST SHEPHERD: We were afraid.

SECOND SHEPHERD: The angel said not to fear; there was good news for us!

THIRD SHEPHERD: That this day was born in the city of David a Savior, who is Christ the Lord.

ALL SHEPHERDS: Now we have come. Now we have found him wrapped in swaddling cloths even as the angel told us. Now we see him in the manger.

FIRST CHILD: Verse 18.

(*Lights out*)

Scene IV: In the stable
   Figure of Mary in profile looking down at baby in manger.

FIRST CHILD: Verse 19. (Pause) Verse 20.

(*Lights out*)

STORIES TO PLAY WITH SHADOW FIGURES

FOR JUNIORS

"By the Side of the Trail" and "Within the Four Seas," from *Many Hands in Many Lands*

"Eyes for Tata Luis," from *The Missionary Story Hour*

PLAY USING MINIATURE FIGURES

Making and manipulating small three-dimensional figures on a table top, sand table, or piano bench stage and speaking lines for them is another way to play a story. People of long ago, people living today, men, women, and children, all can appear in miniature to become the actors, and by their appearance and the conversation of the children who speak for them, whisk the speakers and viewers alike to places near and far, to school or church in their own town or to a place in Alaska or Hawaii.

PRIMARY children especially enjoy this way of playing a story. YOUNGER JUNIORS also may use it sometimes.

CHOOSING THE STORY

Almost any story may be played with miniature figures. The one chosen needs plenty of characters to provide each child with the opportunity to make and to "operate" a figure. Additional conversation may be included so that each character has at least one line to contribute, such as: "Hello," "Good morning," "Where are you going?"

FIGURES TO USE

CLAY. When clay is the medium, each figure requires a ball of clay somewhat larger than a Ping-pong ball. In creating the figures the ball becomes the *body* and *legs,* and the base is kept flat and firm. *Head, arms,* and *feet* are pinched outward from the ball, never stuck on as added pieces. The completed figures should be bulky and massive in form, not thin and fragile.

94

PLAY ACTORS OF PAPER AND CLOTH

Facial features are not necessary to give reality to the figure. Reality is achieved by using poster paints to paint on clothing and a headdress that immediately identify the figure as a Navaho boy, a Spanish dancer, a king, or Little Boy Blue.

A coat of clear shellac applied after the paint dries helps to keep the figure from chipping.

CLOTHESPINS. When clothespins are the medium, each figure is created from one clothespin, not the clip kind. The *head* is made by placing a wad of cotton around the knob of the clothespin, then covering the cotton with a small **square** of white cloth and tying this cloth securely at the "neck" below the knob. *Features,* if added, may be put on with ink or paint, but are not necessary. Two white pipe cleaners twisted firmly around the neck become the figure's *shoulders, arms,* and *hands.*

The figure will stand upright if the base is pushed into a pat of moist clay or into two slits cut in heavy cardboard.

Clothing is made from a discarded sheet or pillowcase. A simple garment is made by cutting a piece of the cloth about three by seven inches and folding it across the center, then cutting a slit part way along the fold to form the neck opening and slipping the head through it.

Dress trimmings are made by crayoned on stripes, borders, flowers, or pasted on designs of metallic paper, beads, or contrasting material.

STORIES TO PLAY WITH FIGURES
    "The Three Surprises," from *The Round Window* (P)
    "The Miracle," from *The Missionary Story Hour* (J)

95

PLAY ON A HANGING STAGE

This kind of play is interesting to both eye and ear because in it children not only talk for the characters, but also move them about on a *vertical* stage that hangs on the wall.

With practice, OLDER PRIMARIES and JUNIORS are able to use this medium satisfactorily.

NEEDED EQUIPMENT

THE HANGING STAGE OR FLANNELBOARD. This is made of beaverboard or wallboard cut about a yard square and covered on one side with outing flannel, nap side out. The leader may secure the materials and the children make the stage by thumbtacking the flannel along the back edge of the board, keeping the flannel smooth and without wrinkles on the front side.

THE FIGURES. To make the figures, the children will draw them on cardboard or Manila tag, "dress" them with paint or crayons on one side, and after pasting outing flannel, nap side out, on the other side, cut out the figures.

THE BACKGROUND. A permanent background of sky and a tree or two may be painted or crayoned directly on the flannel of the stage and each story scene enacted against it. But clouds, sun, stars, paths, mountains, ships, birds, etc., made as separate figures (as above) and put into place as the story progresses offer more opportunities for imaginative work from the children.

PLAY ACTORS OF PAPER AND CLOTH

How to use the equipment

The stage is hung on the wall low enough for the children to reach it easily. The children stand on either side of it and move the figures of people, animals, sky, river, into the desired position against the board while at the same time speaking the dialogue for the characters. The figures' flannel backs being pressed against the flannel of the stage's front causes the figures to remain securely in place to form the scene.

The children's movements in placing the various figures on the stage can become as deft and their arrangements can become quite as interesting as when they use the three-dimensional figures on the horizontal stage.

Younger children, in this kind of play, may prefer to concentrate on the movement of the figures and let the teacher narrate the story.

Stories to play on the hanging stage

FOR PRIMARIES

"My Nipa Hut," from *Second Son*

"One Stone and Another," from *The Missionary Story Hour*

FOR JUNIORS

"The Road to Friendship" and "Making Men Over," from *The Missionary Story Hour*

"The Search Is Ended," from *Ricardo's Search*

Radio and Television Plays

This entire chapter describes ways of story play that are suitable for JUNIORS only.

RADIO

Playing a story the radio way challenges the creative talents of older boys and girls. It is not easy to convey a story's message when the tellers are out of sight. Nor is it easy to make a situation live when players and listeners are hidden from one another. Yet in a radio play, ears and not eyes must be used to receive the story's message. A curtain or folded screen placed between the players and their listeners makes the "broadcasting studio." Thereafter the players must rely on sound alone, since no hand motion, no frown or smile can assist them in their portrayal of the characters.

VOICES

The player's voice is his only personal tool in radio play. He uses its *tone*—high, low, hard, soft—and its *tempo*—hurried, deliberate, halting, lilting—to convey the character's mood, his age, and something of his personality.

He also uses it to simulate other sounds, such as a horse whinnying, a cat meowing, a pig oinking.

RADIO AND TELEVISION PLAYS

SOUND EFFECTS

Improvised sound effects achieved through the children's experimentation help to give reality to their radio plays.

Some are *artificial*, such as the various sounds that may be achieved by

Crumpling cellophane and paper	Rubbing pieces of sandpaper together
Striking metal pans together	Tearing cloth
Rubbing a stick on a washboard	Hammering on wood

Some are *real*, such as

Banging a door	Taking running steps
Opening a window	Cracking nuts
Striking a match	Winding a clock

SELECTING STORIES TO PLAY RADIO FASHION

For obvious reasons, the radio play is an excellent medium for presenting stories whose characters are difficult to portray visually, such as giants, dwarfs, animals, or persons who are very different in one way or another from the actors.

It is useful also for stories that are familiar to the children. The playing of such a story gives additional pleasure to the players, who must create it anew in order to present it in a different medium, and to the listeners, who try to anticipate how certain of the story situations will be devised when they can be only heard, not seen.

TWO SUGGESTIONS FOR INTRODUCING A RADIO PLAY

BY A BOY'S CURIOSITY

A radio play may be introduced quite naturally by a curious boy lounging in an easy chair in his pretend room at home. Consulting a copy of *Radio Guide* he reads aloud several of the program titles, then exclaims

skeptically, " 'New Hands'? Now what kind of accident could a person have had to make him need some new hands? This is something I've gotta hear."

He leans over to the table and turns the dial of the radio. The station identification and the announcer's voice giving a brief résumé of the story come "over the air" from behind the screen, and the drama begins: "New Hands," from *Sidewalk Kids*.

BY A FAMILY'S INTEREST

It also may be introduced by children acting as members of a family who not only have a special interest in the church's missionary work, but also contribute generously to it. The family group is seated in the living room, waiting to hear another in the series of dramatizations describing this work.

Father turns the radio dial. Mother and children look expectantly toward him as he says, "Whatever the story is, I am sure it will make us proud that our church can depend on us to help in its missionary work all over the world."

The station identification comes through, followed by a brief announcement about the program, then the dramatization begins: "A Stick Rubs on Paper," from *Many Hands in Many Lands*.

A STORY TO BE PRESENTED AS A RADIO PLAY

This play, adapted from Chapter 1 of *The Gray Eyes Family,* is a story written for primary age children. Juniors will enjoy the message of the story. They will think it fun to make their voices like those of two-year-old Peaches, of Mary who is six, as well as of junior age Tom and the several adults.

They will be able to bring humor and added lightness to their interpretation of the story situation. They will discover that there are some stories that appeal to all ages.

RADIO AND TELEVISION PLAYS

NARRATOR: Our story today takes place in Navaholand, in the hogan home of Mr. Hasteen Gray Eyes and his wife, Denezbah Gray Eyes. Their children are Tom, so old he has lost count of the years, about ten or eleven; Mary, between six and seven; Peaches, who is two; and just as the story begins there is somebody new in the hogan—so new he does not have any name but Ah-way, which just means "baby."

The time of the story is the Month of Corn Planting— June—the beginning of summer. You now will hear Mr. Gray Eyes speaking to Tom, his son. Other members of the family are with them in the hogan.

FATHER: Tom, put another stick on the fire. (*Sound of crackling paper.*) Ah-way, our baby, looks good lying there on the sheepskin. I think he will grow up to be strong, but we can't always call him Ah-way, the baby.

TOM: Ah-way is no good. He won't help me herd our sheep. (*Sound of laughter.*)

MARY: I'll care for Ah-way, the baby. I think he is all right. But Peaches doesn't like him. Peaches wants to be the baby.

PEACHES: Peaches *is* baby.

(*Sound of creaking of wagon wheels. Extracting nails from a wooden board can be made to give creaking sound.*)

MARY: Can they be here, my mother, the relatives come to see the baby? (*Sound of moccasined feet against floor.*) I'll look out the door; their wagon seems nearby. (*Pause.*) I see them, my mother! They have come, my grandfather and my grandmother and my aunts and my uncles and my brothers and my sisters.

MOTHER: Good! I am glad my people are here. My daughter, these cousins, in our Navaho way, are truly like your brothers and sisters. (*Sounds of footsteps and moving people.*)

GRANDMOTHER: The baby. Where is Ah-way? Bring him to me. (*Footsteps.*) Ah, he is beautiful—*ni-zho-nih.*

GRANDFATHER: Beautiful!

AUNTS AND UNCLES AND COUSINS: Beautiful!

PEACHES: Peaches is beautiful. (*Sound of laughter.*)

GRANDFATHER: My little Peaches, you *are* beautiful, just like a little prairie dog. Let's see how much you have grown. Come, I'll swing you up into the air.

PEACHES: Ow! Ow! (*Sound of laughter.*)

GRANDFATHER: You're too big for me. You make me lose my breath. (*Sound of grandfather huffing and puffing, out of breath.*)

MOTHER: Our baby is two weeks old. He needs a name, a real name, a Navaho name.

FATHER: That is true. The name Ah-way is not enough for him.

GRANDFATHER: I would like to give him my name. I have used it a long time, and it is a good Navaho name. Do you like that?

FATHER: Yes, I like that.

MOTHER: I like it, too.

GRANDFATHER: Then let me hold the baby. It is time, I think.

MOTHER: All right. (*Sound of movement and then sound of baby being patted on back.*)

GRANDFATHER: My grandchild, I give you my true Navaho name. May it keep you from harm. May it help you to live many years. May you always keep it a good name. I now give you this name that is mine—Son-of-One-Who-Catches-Eagles.

MARY: Grandfather, I will put the name far back in my mind and always remember it.

TOM: I will put it far back in my mind and remember it.

PEACHES: Peaches can't remember.

GRANDMOTHER: Son-of-One-Who-Catches-Eagles needs a name for every day. What are you going to call him for every day?

FATHER: I think we are going to call him Sam. That is Trader Sam's name, and it is a good one for every day.

MOTHER: The naming day is an important day. We must eat together in celebration. I will cook coffee. (*Sound of water being poured into the pot.*)

GRANDMOTHER: I will make the bread. (*Sound of piece of clay being slapped between hands.*)

THE AUNTS: We will put the stew on to cook. (*Sound of pans being made ready.*)

MARY: I will fry the bread. (*Sizzling and cooking sounds.*)

NARRATOR: And when the meal was ready, the family sat on the ground near the hogan doorway and ate all the good food. And if you think that because Grandfather gave his name to Ah-way the matter was settled, you are mistaken. Listen next week at this same time, and you will hear more about what happened to Ah-way.

STORIES TO BE PLAYED ON THE RADIO

"The Gift of a Song," from *The Missionary Story Hour* (J)

"Omen and the Jumbies," from *Many Hands in Many Lands* (J)

TELEVISION

Playing a story by television makes the story seem up-to-date, modern, and important. Juniors will find that presenting a story this way may not be as simple as it at first seems, but in the working out of plans there are many opportunities for experimentation and for achieving creative results.

GETTING READY

The television *"screen"* may be simulated by putting up a frame and acting the story within it. To be realistic, the screen should be no larger than the lower half of a window frame.

The *announcer* (unseen) may give the station identification and repeat the title of the story play.

Credits for the play may be printed in large letters on large size cardboard and inserted on the "screen" (the framed opening) to be read by the viewers. Or these names may be read aloud by some member of the class while the printed card remains in place, as:

Title of the play_____

Adapted from the book_____

Producer_____

Director_____

Cast of characters_____

RADIO AND TELEVISION PLAYS

SOME LIMITATIONS OF THE TELEVISION PLAY

- Not every story is suitable for playing the television way because of the limitations of the acting area.

- Not every member of the class can participate at the same time in the play, because no more than three people can squeeze into the frame area at the same time, and then only heads and shoulders can be seen.

- Properties arc limited to those that may be put in view against the wall behind the actors' heads or held up in their hands for the viewers to see.

SUGGESTED TECHNIQUES FOR A TELEVISION PRESENTATION

QUESTIONS AND ANSWERS

The interview type television play may be effective when the group is sharing information about a current study area. One or two panelists appear and are questioned by the interviewer.

Much thought will be needed to state the questions in a clear, concise, crisp manner and to make the replies brief but at the same time interesting and informative. Humor and flashes of wit in both questions and answers bring brightness and sparkle to the story play.

NEWSCAST

One person conducts this program and with a globe, wall maps, pointer, and flat pictures, plus plenty of information, he may present an unusual and informative story. Here also, understanding, wit, and intelligence are needed in the planning.

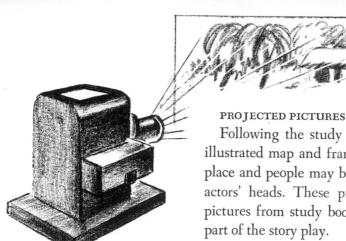

PROJECTED PICTURES

Following the study of a particular place or people, an illustrated map and frames of a filmstrip descriptive of the place and people may be projected on the wall back of the actors' heads. These projected materials, along with flat pictures from study books, are shared with the viewers as part of the story play.

THEATER IN THE ROUND

A "theater in the round" probably is not often used by children as a way of story play, but because it is different it can kindle enthusiasm for this activity when the more ordinary ways do not.

THE STAGE

The middle of the classroom becomes the acting or stage area, and viewers' chairs are arranged to encircle it. Thus, the scene, the actors, and the action are viewed with equal clarity by all.

EXITS

Exits and entrances are no problem. The players may be seated in the first row of chairs that encircle the stage, go onstage from them, and return to them after each exit. Or when aisles are arranged between the viewers' chairs, the actors may enter and exit through them and wait in the rear of the room until time for their next appearance.

RADIO AND TELEVISION PLAYS

PROPERTIES

There are no curtains, no backdrop scenery, no wings. Those properties or movable bits of scenery that are used are simple ones and are put into place between scenes and in full view of the audience. Sometimes dialogue may be included with this activity of placing the properties, and then it becomes incorporated into the play itself.

STORIES FOR READING ALOUD IN THEATER IN THE ROUND
(See Chapter 3, page 36)
"Good-by to the Ozarks," from *Blueberry Acres*
"Better Than the Dream," from *Blueberry Acres*
"Follow the Line," from *Stories of the Book of Books*
"Fight or Shake Hands," from *The Missionary Story Hour*

STORIES THAT MAY BE ACTED IN A THEATER IN THE ROUND
"Seven Pieces of Silk," "The Prize Bible," and "The Dusted Bible,"
all from *Stories of the Book of Books*

10

Choral Speaking

Choral speaking is a group's oral interpretation of their material in poetic rather than narrative or dialogue form. As in other forms of story play, the teacher is always aware of the possibilities offered for the children's growth and is prepared to give inspiration and suggestion when and where needed.

Choral speaking seems suitable for OLDER PRIMARY and JUNIOR children. Both groups are soon surprised by the delight that comes through the using of their words, phrases, and sentences in this interesting way, a way they themselves have planned and arranged.

Speaking in unison is an ancient art. It was part of the life of the people in Bible times, and evidences of it are found in many of the religious and festival ceremonies that are known today. It was part of Greek drama hundreds of years before Jesus lived.

Today, as part of the group worship, members of almost every congregation join together in common prayer and in reading aloud from the Psalms and other portions of the Bible. For many worshipers, the entire service takes on added beauty and significance because of this voicing together of common aspirations and hopes.

108

CHORAL SPEAKING

USE WITH CHILDREN

Children who are members of an orchestra or who sing in a choir already know that skill and practice are needed to blend the instruments or singing tones so that the created sounds are harmonious and pleasing to the ear.

Joining one's voice with other voices to speak in unison also needs skill and practice. But this, too, can be effective and musical and a satisfying way of expressing what one has learned.

MATERIALS TO USE

There is much material both "old" and "new" that may be lifted from current class experiences and lesson material to use in choral speaking form.

OLD MATERIAL, such as

> Selections from the Book of Psalms
> Hymns
> Poems

NEW MATERIAL, such as

> A poem the children have learned
> A song they will sing in a different way
> A story they will tell in a different way
> A summary they will express in short sentences or poetic stanzas
> A biographical portrait of a character they will describe in rhythmic phrases to become the prologue or epilogue of a story play

When children prepare their own material for choral speaking, they understand its context and are able to express it meaningfully, because it comes from their own experience.

PRACTICING

PRINT THE COPY ON THE BLACKBOARD

Children individually or as a group usually are able to follow the leader's directions more readily if they all speak from the same copy of the choral reading, which has been printed on the blackboard or on a large sheet of paper in front of them.

PLAN THE PATTERN

The class will plan the pattern of the choral reading: the lines to be spoken by one, two, three persons, by boys, by girls, by the entire class. Each line, group of lines, or stanza printed on the board is then marked with the speaker's name or initials.

MAKE THE NEEDED CHANGES

Thoughtful practice periods are certain to disclose needed changes: in the word arrangement, in the speakers, in the sequence of speakers. These changes are made as needed and are so indicated on the blackboard copy.

BECOME FAMILIAR WITH THE MATERIAL

Since each child usually has only two or three lines to speak alone, the material becomes familiar, and before the final speaking he usually knows it from memory so that no copy is needed at that time.

HAVE A GOOD TIME

In choral speaking it can be fun to put the voices together in tone and rhythm, then take them apart singly, two by two, three by three, boys' voices, girls' voices, then smoothly join them together again.

CHORAL SPEAKING

It can be fun to place voices in the same key: high, middle, low range; to let them express feelings: sadness, loneliness, fear; to send them out lilting and happy or heavy and dull.

But voices must be ready! Their purpose is to tell the story's message, and lazy, tired, monotonous, singsong, everyday voices will not do!

VALUES OF CHORAL SPEAKING

- It is a tool for learning.

- It is satisfying in and of itself. No audience is needed.

- Yet it may easily be shared, if there is reason for an audience.

- It gives the child encouragement to speak out and not to be afraid of his own voice.

- It provides an opportunity to handle new words.

- It disciplines the child in voice control.

- It emphasizes the total effort rather than the individual contribution.

CHORAL READINGS FOR PRIMARY CHILDREN
"The First Courier," from *The Whole World Singing*

This brief selection is a song poem that tells the story of a wish.

VOICE I, BOY:	I'd love to be a shepherd boy tonight
GROUP VOICES, GIRLS:	Under the open sky.
VOICE I, BOY:	I'd herd my sheep and then I'd watch
GROUP VOICES, BOYS:	The shining stars go by.
GROUP VOICES, GIRLS:	The shining stars go by.
VOICE I, BOY:	And when I saw that wondrous light
	And heard the angels' song,
	I'd hasten into Bethlehem,
GROUP VOICES, SEVERAL BOYS:	Behind the shining throng.

GROUP, REMAINING BOYS:	Behind the shining throng.
VOICE 1, BOY:	I'd follow to the manger
VOICE, SINGLE GIRL:	Where the little Jesus lay,
VOICE 1, BOY:	I'd drop my crook and wallet down
GROUP VOICES, ALL THE BOYS:	So I could kneel and pray.
GROUP VOICES, ALL THE GIRLS:	So I could kneel and pray.

"Worshipers Around the World"

This longer selection summarizes a study unit on churches and tells the story of people who gather for worship.

ALL:	All around the world there are Christian churches,
GIRL A:	Big churches and small,
GIRL B:	Churches under spreading trees, with no building at all.
BOY A:	Churches of bamboo,
BOY B:	Of stone and wood and brick,
GIRL C:	With open roofs and sloping roofs,
GIRL D:	And roofs with snow so thick.
ALL:	People make the churches.
BOYS:	All around the world there are calls to worship on Sunday.
GIRL B:	Bells ringing in towers and steeples,
GIRL C:	Stones striking against iron rods,
BOY C:	Drums beating through the forests,
BOY D:	Records sounding across the valleys,
BOY E:	Antelope horn across the hillsides,
BOY F:	Conch shell beside the sea.
ALL GIRLS:	Boys, girls, fathers, mothers hear the call to worship and come.
ALL:	All around the world these Christian people come.
GIRLS:	From high lands and low lands,
BOYS:	From wet lands and dry lands,
GIRLS:	From hot lands and cold lands.

CHORAL SPEAKING

BOYS:	Christian people of
GIRL D:	All races,
GIRL E:	All colors,
GIRL F:	All ages,
ALL:	Hear the call on Sundays and gather in their places of worship.
ALL GIRLS:	All around the world when Christian people gather for worship,
GIRL A:	They seek knowledge from the Bible,
GIRL B:	Truth from stories and songs.
GIRL C:	They learn about God
GIRL D:	And Jesus, who lived on earth to tell of his love.
GIRL E:	They join one another in friendly fellowship
GIRL F:	To listen, pray, and share.
ALL BOYS:	All around the world people bring their gifts on Sunday,
BOY A:	Gifts of many kinds,
BOY B:	Fruits and grain,
BOY C:	Eggs and chickens,
BOY D:	A pig, a duck, a lamb,
BOY E:	Even a bright new safety pin,
BOY F:	And coins of many sizes.
ALL:	Giving what they need for themselves to others who are in need, too.
ALL:	All around the world Christians sing together,
ALL GIRLS:	"This is the day which the Lord has made; let us rejoice and be glad in it."
ALL:	And they try to remember,
ALL BOYS:	"As you wish that men would do to you, do so to them."
ALL:	All around the world families and friends worship together.

STEPS IN THE DEVELOPMENT OF CHORAL SPEAKING

The teacher motivated class interest for the above reading by suggesting choral speaking as a new and different way to tell the story of their just completed unit on the church.

From the beginning the children planned their choral speaking as part of a service of worship, its purpose to tell the story of worshiping groups around the world.

Since a choral reading is like a poem, the children wanted theirs to include several verses, and they suggested the subjects, which the teacher then printed in large letters on the blackboard:

> Kinds of churches where people worship
> Who the worshipers are
> Where they live
> Ways they are called to worship
> What they do as part of worship
> Ways they share
> Bible verses they know

The children had remembered much information on these subjects from class materials and experiences, such as stories, pictures, filmstrips, visitors, discussions, and they called it out freely to the teacher, who printed each contribution under its proper heading, but with no attempt at order or sequence.

When each verse seemed to be complete, or rather when the children's ideas gave out, the contributions were rearranged to "make sense" and to "sound right."

At first, the entire group read the several verses in unison, but very soon someone suggested that the reading would sound better and be better if individuals read them in turn.

CHORAL SPEAKING

Also that there needed to be a beginning and closing line to each verse. These changes were made and the new method of reading was tried.

By trial and error practices, the children found the right way for both the pattern of the words and for the arrangement of voices. A part of three sessions was needed to reach the "almost completed" form and a part of three more for the completed form. Changes continued until the very last minute, but each change brought improvement.

In the sixth session the reading was shared. The class stood in a semi-circle at the front of the room. The teacher, at their request, stood with them, joined to repeat the lines for "all," and gave encouragement by her presence.

CHORAL READINGS FOR JUNIORS

"Many Hands in Many Lands," from *Many Hands in Many Lands*

This brief selection, arranged from a prose poem, tells the story of hands that do God's work and the lands in which they work.

BOYS AND GIRLS:	God's work needs many hands in many lands.
ALL GIRLS:	God's work needs many hands.
GIRL A:	Healing hands
GIRL B:	Building hands
GIRL C:	Teaching hands
GIRL D:	Laboring hands
GIRL E:	Worshiping hands
GIRL F:	Praying hands
ALL GIRLS:	God's work needs many hands.
ALL BOYS:	In many lands God needs these hands—
BOY A:	In the lands of elephants and teakwood forests
BOY B:	Of rice paddies and rivers
BOY C:	Of donkeys and cornfields
BOY D:	Of blue seas and hummingbirds
BOY E:	Of thatched huts and jungle trails
BOY F:	Of mud walls and mango groves.
ALL BOYS:	In many lands God needs these hands.
BOYS AND GIRLS:	God's work needs many hands in many lands.

"Ships," from *Stories of the Book of Books*

This longer selection is arranged from a poem and tells the story of ships that carry the "good news."

BOY A:	St. Peter pushed his boat out,
BOY B:	The crowds stood held in thrall,
BOY A:	As Jesus sat in the ship and preached
ALL BOYS:	Good news, good news to them all.

Chorus

GIRL A:	From the little sea
	Of Galilee
GIRL B:	Over ocean's widest spaces,

116

CHORAL SPEAKING

GIRL C:	East,
GIRL D:	West,
GIRL E:	South,
GIRL F:	North,
ALL GIRLS:	Good news sped forth
	To the folk of a thousand races.

BOY C:	St. Paul's ship went to the Romans,
BOY D:	Mackey's to Africa's call,
BOY E:	John Williams sailed to the island to take
ALL BOYS:	Good news, good news to them all.

Chorus is repeated as above

BOY A:	From a thousand tribes and peoples,
BOY B:	Boys and girls obey the call.
BOY A:	Sent by a fleet of a thousand ships,
ALL BOYS:	Good news, good news to them all.

GIRL A:	From the little sea
	Of Galilee,
GIRL B:	Over ocean's widest spaces,
GIRL C:	Your ships may reach
GIRL D:	World's ends to preach
GIRL E:	Good news to a thousand races.
BOYS AND GIRLS:	Good news to a thousand races.

OTHER SUGGESTIONS FOR CHORAL SPEAKING
   Bright Pathways, page 6
   Stories of the Book of Books, pages 176 ff.
   The Whole World Singing, pages 17, 78, 117

11

Role Playing

Role playing is the spontaneous, unrehearsed acting out of a situation through conversation and gestures by persons who try to put themselves into another's place in order to better understand that person. Individual A, playing the role of individual B, tries earnestly and honestly to feel as B would feel, to speak the words B would speak, to act as B would act, thereby becoming better able to see and to understand B's side of the situation.

Human relations are always involved in role playing. It is best to avoid the role playing of stories that would arouse deep emotions, since this can sometimes be dangerous to the children taking part.

This type of story play is most suitable for use with JUNIORS.

WHAT TO PLAY

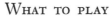

Almost any situation, imagined or real, may be role played, but it becomes more valuable to the group if it is one that is related to the study unit or one that has some bearing on an experience common to the group. It should be one that presents characters with whom the children can readily identify themselves.

118

ROLE PLAYING

Situations that arise from the storybook on a given theme are particularly useful for role playing. One common method is to tell or read the story up to the moment of climax and then have the boys and girls role play what they think might have happened. If the group is large, two or three subgroups may be formed. Each discusses together what they think may have happened or should have happened in the story, and then they act it out, after which the story is completed and its ending compared with the one suggested in the role playing. This method makes the characters in the story come alive for the children.

WHO PLAYS

JUNIOR boys and girls or the teacher or both may suggest the situation to be played. The number of players depends on the type of situation.

WHERE TO PLAY

Role playing may be done any place. No special properties are needed, but some leaders feel that the playing becomes more realistic to the children if the actual environment of the scene can be simulated.

For example, if the situation to be played involves a mother and her child's fifth grade teacher, a desk, blackboard, and table with books and world globe would make the school scene more realistic.

THE TIME NEEDED

This depends on the situation to be played and on other factors, such as the group's interest and participation. The role playing may come to an end naturally or be stopped by the leader as soon as the point is made. It needs to be stopped if the children run out of dialogue or begin to repeat themselves or to lose interest.

Playing the role

After a presentation of the situation, it is discussed, and anyone having a suggestion about the interpretation of a particular role is free to offer it. Then roles are assigned, chosen, or taken in turn, with first one member of the group, then another assuming a particular one. Before the acting begins the teacher will briefly review the situation, remind each child of his role, and allow a few moments for him to get into it, to think about the character, his feelings, his appearance, his speech, his actions, in relation to the situation.

Suggestions about the way the roles are to be played are never offered by the leader. The manner of development and the outcome depend entirely on the children's point of view about the roles they play.

Thus, when the same situation is role played by three different groups, three different outcomes are to be expected. And when the players in a second playing of a situation reverse their roles to take the other side, each one probably will interpret this role quite differently from the preceding player.

Values of role playing

- Role playing gives opportunity for participation by every member of the group.

- It develops skill in sensing another person's feelings.

- It encourages positive changes in attitudes.

- It enables an individual to show how he would handle a particular situation instead of just telling how it ought to be handled.

ROLE PLAYING

Two situations for role playing

SITUATION I

Following a discussion about personal and professional qualifications needed by missionaries who serve the church in other lands, one junior group set up the following situation to role play.

The agricultural missionary is having a hard time persuading the people to use his tested corn seeds rather than those from their own low producing plants. How can he successfully approach the people who so greatly need his services, yet who remain hostile to him? How can he win their co-operation?

Characters

> THE AGRICULTURAL MISSIONARY: who is now in his second year in the area.
>
> FARMER A: who never sees good in any change. "My father always did it this way, so what he did is good enough for me."
>
> FARMER B: who believes nothing good ever comes from another country.
>
> FARMER C: who can't discover why his crops have failed in alternate years. He is willing to listen to the missionary, but is doubtful of receiving any help.
>
> FARMER D: who has heard from neighbors about their good crops after following the missionary's instructions. He is eager to talk to the missionary in person and to ask many questions. Through a friend he has sent word asking the missionary to stop at his farm, and the

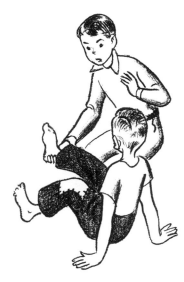

neighbors, seeing the station wagon and being curious, soon appear on the scene.

Scene: In the farmyard of Farmer D

The missionary has tree seedlings, eggs, chickens, corn seed, wire netting for chicken coops, and so forth in his station wagon.

Time: Early morning

SITUATION II

Following their study unit on "Migrant Workers" the junior group wondered what might happen if a committee from their church went to the manager of the migrant camp near their town and tried to persuade him to provide better living conditions for the workers. They would role play the situation.

Characters

THE MANAGER OF THE MIGRANT CAMP

TWO BOARD MEMBERS of the church, appointed to visit the camp, talk to the manager, and do whatever they can to better the living conditions of the workers.

MIGRANT WORKER, a father, who has lately arrived at this camp. His little boy has a serious cut on his foot, received when he stepped on bits of broken glass and tin cans that littered the area. There is no doctor near by to examine the foot, and it seems to be infected.

MIGRANT WORKER, an old man, who worked at this same camp a year ago and says his wages here are a bit higher than on some other jobs, but that this is no advantage to him since he has to pay more for the shack assigned to him for living quarters.

MIGRANT WORKER, a mother, who has just arrived with her family. She is anxious to know if there is a play center at the camp where she may leave her two small children during the day while she and her husband are in the fields at work.

MISSIONARY who has arrived to open the play center to which the manager has finally consented after three years of opposition.

Scene: In the manager's office

Time: Afternoon, a few hours after the arrival of several truckloads of new workers, when the manager is busy, bossy, and bothered

12

Festivals and Games

FESTIVALS

Holidays, festivals, special days, whether known and loved in one country or many, are made more meaningful for children by the use of appropriate stories. And when children *play* the stories of these special days they come to understand something of why the day is a happily celebrated and honored one, to feel a kinship with the children of the particular country that celebrates it.

WHAT FESTIVALS TO PLAY

A list of stories, pictures, and songs that carry the message of holidays, festivals, and special days is given below. Letters in parentheses indicate age level.

NEW YEAR'S DAY
"Putting Up New Year Greetings"—*Children and Their Homes Around the World* (K)
"Happy New Year"—*The Whole World Singing* (P, J)

PALM SUNDAY
"A Song of Praise"—*Children at Worship Around the World* (K)

FESTIVALS AND GAMES

"The Palm Sunday Play"—*The Round Window* (P)

EASTER

"The Easter Song"—*The Missionary Story Hour* (P)
"On Mars Hill"—*Many Hands in Many Lands* (J)

CHILDREN'S DAY

"Peanuts for Church"—*The Round Window* (P)
"God's Gift to Paquito"—*The Singing Secret* (P)
"The Independent Hen"—*Many Hands in Many Lands* (J)
"The Tanbark Church"—*The Missionary Story Hour* (J)

THANKSGIVING

"Caring for the Harvest"—*Children and Their Homes Around the World* (K)
"Sung at Harvest Time"—*The Whole World Singing* (P, J)
"A First Thanksgiving"—*The Round Window* (P)
"Ramón's Hat"—*The Missionary Story Hour* (J)

CHRISTMAS

Rosita: a Little Girl of Puerto Rico (K. See page 58 for dramatization)
"Making Ready for Christmas" and "Hanging the Christmas Wreath"—*Children and Their Homes Around the World* (K)
"Come to Christmas"—*The Missionary Story Hour* (P)
"The Lights of Christmas"—*The Round Window* (P)
"The Singing Secret"—*The Singing Secret* (P)
"Only a Stable"—*Many Hands in Many Lands* (J)

125

"Merry Christmas," "The Little Jesus," "The Christ Child's Stable,"
"Birthday Presents," and "Christmas in Mexico"—*The Whole World Singing* (P, J)
"The Congo Wise Man"—*The Missionary Story Hour* (J)
"The Old Story in a New Land"—*We Gather Together* (J)

CHANUKAH
"Chanukah"—*The Whole World Singing* (P, J)

GAMES

To play a game is to "act it out." When children play colorful games that are known and enjoyed by boys and girls in other lands, it is another way of putting themselves in the places of the faraway children and experiencing their feelings of delight and joy as they sing, dance, skip, and run.

WAYS TO USE THE GAMES
- As interesting information to enrich the study or to use in an extra session as described on pages 129-133

- For fun and pleasure on Family Nights

- As something to share by teaching it to another class

- As part of a service of worship to bring appreciation of this gift from another country

- As an effective program, complete in itself

- As a colorful contribution to a "Friends Around the World" program

GAMES FOR A "FRIENDS AROUND THE WORLD" PROGRAM
(These four games are all found in *Children's Games from Many Lands*)

126

FESTIVALS AND GAMES

STICK DANCE (India)

The announcer, a child, introduces the games: "All around the world children play games and have fun together. This afternoon we invited you to go with us to far-away places to see the children in their games. Our first stop is India, in the courtyard of the mission school. The girls you see are about to begin a favorite game, 'Stick Dance.' Notice that each girl wears a pretty sari. Each holds a pair of brightly colored sticks and stands with her partner in the circle."

The players may hold the pose in tableau for a few moments, then begin the game.

LITTLE HANS (Germany)

The announcer: "Now we are in a park playground in Germany. Please meet the characters of our play:

> Little Hans with his hat and stick
> Hans's Mother
> Hans's Sister
> Hans's Three Neighbors
> The Children."

As each character is named he may come forward and bow or do whatever action has been previously planned. The group then takes its place in the circle and holds the pose a few minutes before beginning the action song as described in *Children's Games from Many Lands*.

CHICKEN MARKET (Italy)

The announcer: "The scene of this game is the chicken market in Italy. Notice carefully and you will discover a new way to pick the finest and fattest chickens for your family's dinner. The characters are:

> The Market Woman
> The Buyer
> The Chickens."

The characters will acknowledge the introduction in whatever way that seems natural, then take their places ready for the dialogue and action as described in the book. Only one or two chickens need to be bought to give the idea of the game.

THE FOUNTAIN (Cuba)

The announcer: "Now we come to Cuba and 'La Fuente,' the fountain. Notice the high arch the leaders form with their upraised arms and the pretty line of girls, each holding to the bright, full-gathered skirt of the friend in front of her. Listen to their song and you will hear what happens to the fountain."

The girls, as the announcer speaks, may form the arch and start through it, then hold the pose a moment before beginning their skipping. The game may close when the first girl is caught under the arch.

FESTIVALS AND GAMES

FESTIVALS AND GAMES COMBINED

Teachers—children, too—often are concerned because there is so *little* time in the class session, yet so much to teach and to learn. When the teachers are concerned enough to do something about it, they are likely to come up with a wonderful, workable idea that may be used with variations for years and years.

The extra session described below is such an idea, permitting several hours of extra learning and fun for the children and enabling the teacher to present and use a variety of enriching materials supplementing those already presented in the class period . . . and to see the results.

Such a session will be planned by teachers and all the children, smaller committees working on special assignments, such as tickets, painting the ship for background interest, making the hot chocolate, collecting the properties for the four "corner groups," and so forth.

The idea of course may be applied to the study of any country.

A STORY PLAY IN AN EXTRA SESSION

THE INVITATION

"Come aboard the SS *World Friends*

Sailing time: Saturday morning, 10:30

Place: Pier 31 (Maple Street Community Church)

Destination: India. Passports not required

Cost: 25 cents

Ship returns: 3:00 P.M.

Baggage needed: Box lunch for noon meal. Hot chocolate served aboard

Dress: Bluejeans and T shirts."

SHIPBOARD EVENTS

Buying tickets. Each child stops at the booth inside the church door and in exchange for 25 cents receives a ticket, long, short, pink, green, complicated, or simple, as planned by the committee. This money becomes the children's contribution toward a gift for the church's work in India.

All Aboard! At three blasts of the whistle the children go into the assembly hall and up the gangplank to find a place on deck (the stage). The ship, with its name in big letters on the side (painted in class by a committee) is tacked to the back stage wall and helps provide "sea" atmosphere.

On deck. The children with the help of the deck steward (the teacher) trace their route to India on a large map or globe to discover how far it is, what countries they pass, etc. Those who know interesting information about India share it. They may play an American game and sing an American song which they will later teach to the friends they will meet in India.

The travelers plan their sight-seeing. In India each of the groups of children with its leader must learn one special thing about India and find a way to share it on the return trip, such as:

      Indian homes
      An Indian Christian church
      A school and games
      An Indian *mela* (festival)

Lunch time. The children have their lunch together and take a rest on deck.

All Ashore! The assembly room becomes the land of India, and each group with its leader proceeds to tour the country, that is, to go to the particular corner of the room that is prepared for its activity.

FESTIVALS AND GAMES

GROUP 1. The girls put on saris and the boys put on turbans, and they become the Indian family. Their home is a paneled screen covered with white paper and folded to form the outside wall (see Settings: A Screen, page 48).

Seated beside the wall they listen as the teacher tells the story "Making Ready for Christmas," from *Children and Their Homes Around the World.* The children then dramatize the story. They make the clay lamps and pretend to light them before putting them in place; they cut brightly colored paper pennants and hang them across the "yard." The mother paints a Christmas scene on the white walls of the house. There may be other activities also. Each child takes his clay lamp back to America as a souvenir.

GROUP 2. This group also puts on turbans and saris. The church is another screen covered with white paper and folded so three panels become the back and two sides, leaving the front open. Seated inside the church the children hear the story "The Church That Was Builded by Moonlight," from *We Gather Together,* as told by the teacher in the role of minister-missionary.

The children dramatize the story by painting the church to resemble the open brickwork shown in the story's illustration. A brief litany, prayer, or song of praise concludes the dedication of the church. Each child prints a copy of this for his souvenir.

GROUP 3. This group attends an outdoor school beneath a mango tree. The tree previously painted in a class session is now attached to a wall at the side of the room. The children sit beside it, girls in saris and boys in turbans. Pieces of beaverboard or heavy cardboard become the writing boards and black crayons the pencils. The teacher teaches a Bible verse, which the children copy and keep for their souvenir.

If there is time a game may be learned and played. The two suggested are from *Children's Games from Many Lands.*

The Lion and the Goat
Who Is It?

GROUP 4. This group attends a Christian *mela,* an Indian festival.

The merchants' booths are boxes or cartons with pretend wares spread out over the tops; the merchants are the children with turban headdresses.

The leafy huts where the Christian people sleep are made of chairs with rugs draped over them. In one booth the Christian leader gives Bible leaflets and pictures to the children; in another a Christian leader tells Bible stories to them.

An oxcart bringing a family to the *mela* is made by tacking large cardboard cutout wheels to a low table, then tacking a strip of corrugated cardboard around three sides of the table to become the stand-up sides of the cart. The family sitting inside the cart and the cart itself are decorated with flower chains, and a flower chain is the souvenir taken home by each member of this group.

All Aboard Again! Back on the ship's deck again, each group reports where it has been, what it has seen, what it has learned, and shows its souvenirs. If time permits, everyone joins to play one of the Indian games.

HOME!
Down the gangplank, off the pier to meet families and friends and to share with them the day's adventures.

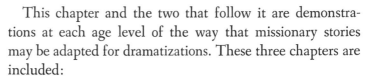

A Kindergarten Story to Play

ADAPTING STORIES FOR PLAYING

This chapter and the two that follow it are demonstrations at each age level of the way that missionary stories may be adapted for dramatizations. These three chapters are included:

- To stimulate the teacher's interest in playing a story by providing material that is ready to use.

- To show the "mechanics" of adapting a story for story play so that leaders will be encouraged to try adaptations of the children's favorite stories.

- To make the point that within all missionary materials are purposes other than the specific missionary emphases and that these materials may be appropriately presented any day of the year, because the characteristics they present are universal. They show that:

> The feeling of wanting to share with others something that you yourself like does not belong exclusively to any one race or culture or age group. It is found everywhere—in the Philippines, in Africa—as well as in our own country.

A KINDERGARTEN STORY TO PLAY

The message of love finds expression in many ways, in many places. It is not confined to any one person in any one country. A toyshop keeper in India has it. A Japanese child has it.

People—wherever they live—work hard for that which seems important to them. Christian villagers in India cannot afford to pay for what they want, but by every village family working together, they manage to secure it.

JUAN AND JUANITA

This delightful story by Sara Klein (see page 161) describes a Filipino family who travel from their home in the country to their cousins' home in the city to take presents. Because giving presents and receiving them are experiences every child likes, the story will be played with enjoyment and understanding.

In the *first telling*, the children will listen and will imagine the action.

In the *first playing*, while the teacher retells the story, the children will spontaneously participate when they want to and in the way they want to. Because of the frequent repetition of the refrain, some children may begin at once to join in repeating it each time. In a *later playing*, the children may point out certain places in the room to become the two homes, the cart, the bus, with particular members of the class becoming the various story people and the monkey, horse, dog, chicken. Instead of there being just two cousins, as in the story, the play may have six or seven or more cousins.

In the adapted text below, certain action words are italicized, as suggested clues for the children's action responses. The children may think of others.

The story is arranged in "paragraphs" as guides to the leader for pauses in the narration to wait for the children's participation.

NARRATOR: Juan and Juanita are twins. They live with Papá, Mamá, and Baby Charing in a country house in the Philippines. Tony, their pet monkey, lives in a tree nearby, and he and the children *peek at each other* through the trees, then *run away and hide* (pause).

(Continuing after pause)
One day Papá *says* to the family, "Let's take a trip to the city to visit Uncle Bernardo, Aunt Maria, and the cousins." Juan and Juanita like the idea very much. They *clap their hands* and *dance round and round* (pause).

Mamá *says*, "Let's take presents. I'll take a pretty white cloth for Aunt Maria."

Papá *says*, "I'll get bananas to take for Uncle Bernardo."

Juan and Juanita *say*, "We'll take good bukayo (boo-kye-oh) candy for the cousins."

They *bring their presents* and *give them* to Papá and *help him put them in a big cloth* to make a big bundle (pause).

Then Papá holding the bundle and Mamá holding Baby Charing *go outside* with Juan and Juanita and *climb into the cart*. And they all *wave* to their friends and neighbors (pause).

A KINDERGARTEN STORY TO PLAY

Papá *calls* out to friends and neighbors, "Good day to you. We're going to visit cousins."

Juan *says,* "We're taking presents . . . bananas . . ."

Juanita *says,* "And a pretty white cloth . . ."

And Juan and Juanita *say together,* "And good bukayo candy!"

And in the cart they *go jogging along, jogging along* to the city (pause).

In the city, Papá *takes the horse* to the stable, and Mamá, Baby Charing, and Juan and Juanita *climb out of the cart* and *walk down one street,* then another street, and when they come to the bus stop they all *climb inside the bus* and *sit down* (pause).

Papá *comes,* too, and *sits down.* He holds the bundle. Mamá holds Baby Charing.

Papá *speaks* to the bus driver, "Good day to you. We're going to visit cousins."

Juan *says,* "We're taking presents . . . bananas . . ."

Juanita *says,* "And a pretty white cloth . . ."

And Juan and Juanita *say together,* "And good bukayo candy!"

And they *ride* and *ride* until the bus stops at the right corner. Then they all *get off,* Papá, Mamá, Baby Charing, Juan, and Juanita. And they *walk* and *walk,* and Juan and Juanita *run* and *run* to the cousins' house (pause).

Papá *says,* "Good day to you! We've come for a visit."

Juan *says,* "We've brought presents . . . bananas . . ."

Juanita *says,* "And a pretty white cloth . . ."

And Juan and Juanita *say together,* "And good bukayo candy!"

And Uncle Bernardo and Aunt Maria and all the cousins are so pleased they *hop* and *skip* and *dance* (pause).

Uncle Bernardo and Aunt Maria *say,* "Welcome to our house."

Papá *places the bundle* on the floor, and he *unties* the string and *takes out* the yellow bananas and the pretty white cloth. But . . . the good bukayo candy is NOT there!

Juan and Juanita and all the cousins *begin to cry,* and they *cry louder* and *louder* (pause).

Then there is *a knock at the door.* It is the bus driver, and he is *holding a package.* Juan and Juanita and all the cousins *stop their crying.* Everyone *runs to the door* to see who is there (pause).

138

A KINDERGARTEN STORY TO PLAY

The bus driver *holds out* the package. "You left this in my bus. I think it fell out of the big bundle."

Juan *cries out*, "The good bukayo candy!"

Juanita *cries out*, "The good bukayo candy!"

Everyone *tells* the bus driver thank you, and Aunt Maria *opens* the package and *passes the candy* to each person.

Everyone *takes a piece* and *is very happy.*

14

A Story Play by Primary Children

THE THREE CAMELS

This story tells the adventures of three toy camels and the three children who found them in a toyshop in India, and the wonderful story the camels helped to bring to the children.

Though *The Three Camels* (see page 161) was written for kindergarten children, it was happily played by a first grade as part of a December service of worship and was happily enjoyed by second and third grade children. Its message is for all ages.

ADAPTATIONS

Because the group numbered more boys than girls, the story's "Susie" became the play's "Tom." And, in order to give an acting part to each member of the group, children not in the story's text were included in the play as additional visitors to the toyshop.

SCENERY AND PROPERTIES

To eliminate curtain pulling between scenes, both scenes were in full view on the low stage during the entire play.

The *toyshop* was at stage right, an India print draped across the corner walls. Appropriate toys, as many as the children and teacher could collect, were hung up to show against the print and were displayed on two tables, a piano bench, and a footstool arranged in tier effect to resemble shelves.

The three camels, large, middle-sized, small, which the children had drawn, painted, cut out, and mounted to stand up, were in prominent places on the bottom shelf.

In *Tom's living room* at stage left were two chairs, some playing blocks on the floor, on the wall a picture of the Three Wise Men riding their camels.

Beneath the picture was a low bench.

A light was directed on the toyshop for Scene I, then changed in position to shine on Tom's living room for Scene II.

THE NARRATOR

The teacher, as narrator, stood on the floor to the right of the stage and paused in the narration while the children spoke their own lines at the appropriate time.

THE PLAYERS

The children sat in their regular places—the first row of chairs—and came to the stage whenever it was their turn to take part, then returned to their places when their parts were completed.

THE BEGINNING OF THE PLAY

As the story play began, the shopkeeper went to his shop as if at the beginning of the day and arranged his toys this way and that, as if he expected customers soon. He was especially particular about the arrangement of the three camels, making certain they were in position to be seen by everyone.

NARRATOR: Once upon a time in India there were three toy camels painted yellow and black and green—a big camel, a middle-sized camel, and a very little camel.

They all stood in a row on the shelf of a very little shop. The shop was kept by a very old man with a very bright smile. (*This was plainly seen by all the audience!*) In his shop there were lots of toys to sell—drums, dolls, rattles, balls, pretty boxes—but the old man liked the three camels best, and he kept them on the front shelf for all to see. Today the old man was happier than usual, for although it was yet early in the morning, he saw coming toward his shop a little girl and her nurse. (*The girl and nurse come from their places in their chairs with their group.*) The little girl was dressed in green and gold, and she had a gold chain around her neck and gold bangles around her arms, and her cheeks were a lovely brown color. Her name was Sita.

When she saw the old man in his shop, she smiled at him. And when she saw the three camels all in a row she stopped and clapped her hands (*action*) and cried:

A STORY PLAYED BY PRIMARY CHILDREN

SITA: Oh, Nurse, please buy me a camel. Oh, please. I want the beautiful big one.

NARRATOR: So Sita and her nurse looked at the camels on the shelf, and the nurse said:

NURSE: Thank you, shopkeeper. We will take this one.

NARRATOR: And the nurse handed some coins to the old man in payment (*nurse does this*), and Sita said to him:

SITA: Oh, thank you for my beautiful big camel!

NARRATOR: Sita took the big camel and tucked it under her arm, and she and the nurse went home.

(*Nurse and Sita exit back to places in chairs.*)

NARRATOR: And then there were only two painted camels left on the shelf. The warm sun shining down on the old man made him sleepy, and while he sat by the door, he fell asleep. (*This action is done by the shopkeeper.*) It wasn't for long, because a shrill little voice soon woke him up. (*Boy Tom approaches shop with mother.*)

TOM: Oh, those cute camels!

NARRATOR: When the old man opened his eyes, he saw it was a little boy and his mother standing in front of his shop. The little boy wore blue pants and a white shirt, and his cheeks were rosy pink. And his name was Tom. Tom pointed to the middle-sized camel and cried:

TOM: Mother, buy it! Buy it! Please, buy it!

NARRATOR: So his mother bought it. (*Mother gives payment to man.*) And Tom said:

TOM: Oh, thank you very much!

NARRATOR: And Tom tucked the middle-sized camel under his arm (*he does this*) and he and his mother went home.

(*Tom and Mother go back to places.*)

And then there was only one little camel left on the shelf. And the shopkeeper looked at the one little camel and said:

SHOPKEEPER: Poor little camel. I'm afraid you'll be lonely by yourself.

NARRATOR: But he did not have long to think about the little camel for all that day other children came to his shop. One bought a drum. (*Child comes and looks around at the toys, picks out the drum, pays the old man, and leaves.*)
Another bought a top (*action the same*).
Another bought a rattle (*action the same*).
Another bought a ball (*action the same*).
Another bought some marbles (*action the same*).
Another came, but he saw nothing he liked so he went home without a toy (*action*).
No one bought the littlest camel. It stayed there on the shelf all by itself.
Finally the shopkeeper got hungry. He said:

SHOPKEEPER: I must go home. My wife will be waiting for me. I will lock my shop so it will be safe.

NARRATOR: Then before he could lock the shop, there beside the shelf stood a tiny little girl—all by herself. She was looking right at the littlest camel. She said not a word, only looked. Then

she put out her hand, but it was an empty hand. There was no money in it. The old man smiled at the tiny little girl and said:

SHOPKEEPER: Why, one little camel for one little girl!

NARRATOR: And he picked up the little camel and put it right into the little girl's hand (*action*). And she hugged the camel and ran away. (*Child runs back to her place.*) And the old man looked around his shop again and made sure that everything was safe, and then he locked it and went away. (*Action. Here the narrator pauses, and the light that had been focused on the shop at the right side of the stage is moved to shine on the left side and Tom's living room.*)

NARRATOR CONTINUES: Now the very next day, in a corner of Tom's living room, Mother sat by the window. Tom played with his blocks and built a house for the middle-sized camel (*action*). And while he worked, he heard someone coming up the steps. He went to the window and looked out (*action*). And he saw his friend Sita coming to play with him. Once every week Sita's nurse brought her to play with Tom, and this was the day. And when they came in the door Tom was surprised. Why, Sita had a camel, too! She was carrying it under her arm. Tom cried:

TOM: Oh, I have a camel, too. My camel's name is George. What is the name of your camel?

SITA: My camel is Ginger.

NARRATOR: And Sita put Ginger in the block house with George. And the nurse sat by the window with Mother, while the children played. And while Tom and Sita played together, Tom's

145

daddy came home from his work in the hospital. (*Enter Father.*) And he looked at George and Ginger and then spoke to the children:

FATHER: Oh-ho! Would you like another camel?

NARRATOR: Daddy got down on his hands and knees (*action*). And Tom put a pillow on his back for a hump (*action*). And Sita climbed up for a ride (*action*). How they all laughed (*action*)! And then Sita's nurse said:

NURSE: It is late, we must go home.

NARRATOR: So the nurse took Sita by the hand (*action*), and in the other hand Sita held Ginger, and they waved good-by (*action*) as they went away home. Then Father sat down (*action*) in the big chair with Mother on one arm of the chair and Tom on the other, and Father said:

FATHER: Christmas will soon be here. It is our first Christmas in India. We will think again of the Three Kings who came riding to see the baby. (*Family turns to look at picture on wall.*) What shall we have for Christmas?

NARRATOR: Tom jumped off the chair and began to dance a jig, he was so happy (*action*). He told Father:

TOM: A tree! A real Christmas tree! Oh, please may we have a tree and ask Sita to come and see the tree?

NARRATOR: Mother and Daddy nodded yes (*action*), then everyone went off to dream about all the fun of Christmas. (*Family exits. During the pause that followed the parent helper came onto the stage and set into place a Christmas tree which the children had painted on paper, decorated with a star, candles, many painted balls, and other ornaments, and had attached to a coat rack [see Chapter 4, Properties: Trees, page 51], so it was easy to carry and to set beside the wall near the Three Kings' picture.)*

NARRATOR CONTINUES: When Christmas Day came, there was a beautiful Christmas tree in Tom's living room, a tree with sparkling candles and bright decorations and a great shining star on top. And the family's favorite Christmas picture which they had brought from America was on the wall nearby, the picture of the Three Wise Men who came on their camels to bring presents to the Baby Jesus.

And that afternoon Tom brought George and came to play beside the tree. (*Enter Tom, who plays under the tree with George and toys.*) Sita came with Ginger. (*Enter Sita.*) Sita asked:

SITA: Where is your mother?

NARRATOR: Tom called, "Mother," and Mother came to sit by the pretty tree. (*Mother enters.*)

NARRATOR: Then Sita said:

SITA: Where is your daddy?

NARRATOR: And Tom answered:

TOM: He is at the hospital taking care of a sick man. I wish he would hurry and come home, because it's Christmas.

NARRATOR: Just then the door opened and there was Daddy, and close beside him was a very little brown girl (*action*). And Daddy said:

147

FATHER: This is Sakena, whose father is sick in our hospital. She is going to stay with us until her father gets well.

NARRATOR: And Tom and Sita were so surprised they could say nothing for almost a whole minute. For the little girl Sakena was hugging the very little camel that had been in the toy man's shop! Then Sita cried:

SITA: Oh! Oh! Oh!

NARRATOR: And Tom said:

TOM: What's *your* camel's name?

NARRATOR: And Sakena said:

SAKENA: My camel's name is Gunga.

NARRATOR: Then Sakena saw the pretty tree, and she went close to it and looked at all the pretty balls and shining decorations (*action*). And Mother told the children:

MOTHER: Put all your camels on the bench under the Christmas picture of the camels, the big one, the middle-sized one, the little one (*action*). Then come and sit on the floor by my chair, and I will tell you the story of those camels that brought the Wise Men to see the Baby Jesus (*action*).

NARRATOR: And while the children listened, this is the story they heard: "Now when Jesus was born in Bethlehem of Judea in the days of Herod the king, behold, wise men from the East came to Jerusalem, saying, 'Where is he? . . . We have seen his star in the East, and have come to worship him.'

"When Herod the king heard this . . . he sent the wise men to Bethlehem. . . . They went their way; and lo, the star

148

which they had seen in the East went before them, till it came to rest over the place where the child was. When they saw the star, they rejoiced exceedingly with great joy; and going into the house they saw the child with Mary his mother, and they fell down and worshiped him. Then, opening their treasures, they offered him gifts, gold and frankincense and myrrh. And . . . they departed to their own country."

After the story Tom, Sita, and Sakena went and stood by the picture (*action*). They looked at their three camels on the bench (*action*). They looked at the three camels in the picture (*action*). They said to Ginger and George and Gunga:

THE THREE CHILDREN SPEAK: Oh, hasn't it been a happy Christmas!

NARRATOR: And everybody took hands and all danced around the Christmas tree, for indeed it had been a very happy Christmas. (*Action. The children then leave platform and return to places.*)

15

A Junior Story Play

THE CHURCH THAT WAS BUILDED
BY MOONLIGHT

This moving story, from *We Gather Together* (see page 161), is an account of the determination of an Indian Christian group to have a church of their own and how they persisted in it until the church was built, in spite of a seemingly impossible hindrance.

The story play was developed by juniors in a vacation school.

ADAPTATIONS

Because there were more girls than boys in the class, a "wise old woman" spoke the lines of the "wise old man."

A character, "the pessimist," was added, also action not in the story was invented and dramatically strengthened the play's scenes.

CHILDREN'S RESPONSIBILITIES

In addition to preparing the story play's dialogue, the children planned and made the simple scenery, properties, and costumes.

A JUNIOR STORY PLAY

Scene I is here presented in detail as this group developed it.

Scenes II, III, and IV are presented in sufficient detail to enable other groups to complete them in their own way.

Scene I: A clearing at the edge of a village in India

> Trees painted on large sheets of paper are hung against the wall as background.
>
> At the side and front of the stage are stacks of bricks made from empty shredded wheat boxes, filled with sand, covered with newspapers, and painted red. This exaggeration of the brick size is important: ordinary bricks are much too small for a dramatic effect.
>
> As the scene opens, two "children" play jacks at one side of the stage.
>
> Two others roll a ball between them.
>
> At the other side of the stage one "woman" is busy with colored threads, embroidering a piece of cloth. Another, with a container of water and clay beside her, painstakingly shapes the clay into a pretty bowl.
>
> A "man" carves a piece of wood.
>
> Raj-Singh, the preacher-teacher, and two other "men" are stacking the bricks in orderly fashion and seem to be counting them.

Two more "women," carrying water jars as if on their way home from the village well, enter the scene. They pause near the two "women" who are working and then look with interest towards Raj-Singh and his helpers as they stack the bricks. Finally one of the women speaks.

WOMAN WITH WATER JAR: Is it true that at last all the bricks are made? That at last we can build our church?

WOMAN WITH EMBROIDERY: Yes, what you have heard is true. See? I work each day so that this cloth will be finished for the altar of our church.

WOMAN WITH CLAY: My bowl will also soon be finished. Into it will go the first offering when we meet together in the new church.

RAJ-SINGH (*speaking so all can hear*): How long we have waited! For months and months I, your preacher and teacher, have thought and prayed about this church we Christians have hoped and worked for. At last the ground is bought, the bricks made. In only a short while now, the church will be ready for our first service.

MAN: We have waited so long!

WOMAN: We have worked so hard!

SECOND MAN: It is worth our work and waiting. Our church will be beautiful, and soon we shall see it standing right here where we now are.

WOMAN: We women will work to beat the earthen floor and make it smooth and even.

A JUNIOR STORY PLAY

MAN: We men will lay the bricks carefully. The low walls will keep the cows and dogs from straying inside.

WOMAN: Even the children will do what they can to help in the building.

SECOND MAN: The bricks of the side walls we will set wide apart like a lattice to let the stray breezes come through to cool us. The bricks of the end wall we will make to rise higher than the others.

RAJ-SINGH: That wall will be solid, with openings in the bricks to make the design of a cross. When the light shines through it, the cross design will be before us, the symbol of our Christian faith. All who see it will know that this church is our house of praise. Yes, we shall have our church at last, where we can worship in our own way.

PESSIMIST: Why are you so sure we will have it? We have tried to build a Christian church many times. Always there is trouble. First we could not get straw for our bricks. Then the rains came, and we could not work. I say it is better not to hope too much. Something will happen this time, too. It always has before.

RAJ-SINGH: This time our bricks are ready. The rainy season is over. The hands of the Christians in the village are ready to work. No, there is nothing more to fear. Tomorrow we shall meet here again. We shall work in the cool of the morning. We shall have our church.

(The group join to sing a simple melody, such as "Our Faith Is Such a Glorious Thing," then slowly move off stage together.)

Scene II: In the clearing

The painted backdrop shows the back brick wall under construction, reaching two to three feet high, the bricks painted red and matching the size of the shredded wheat "bricks," with division markings of white.

The same group meet as planned and are happily at work when the Hindu priest and landlord appear. The landlord hurls his threat: "There will be no Christian place of worship built. It is my order. If any building is done, I will have my young men tear down each night that which you have built each day. Save yourselves the trouble."

The pessimist grumbles, "I told you! Trouble has come again just as I predicted."

The Christians, discouraged, slowly leave the scene. Raj-Singh calls them back. He is certain that a way can be found to build the church in spite of the threats. The pessimist sees no hope. The others are inclined to agree with him. Raj-Singh, however, will not give up.

"Have patience," he tells the people. "If there is a law to protect the priest, there must be a law to protect the Christian. I must find that law."

Scene III: The several places that Raj-Singh visits in search of a law that will help

Across the stage four folding screens (see Settings, page 48) are arranged, each to become a house, with two side walls, a rear wall, and the front open. One house at extreme left, another at extreme right, the others in between, spaced as far as possible one from the other, as if in separate villages.

154

In each house a "lawyer" sits on a mat with many books around him. Raj-Singh travels from one village to the second, to the third, seeking out the wise man in each village, explaining to each in turn the Christians' problem, and asking for help. Each lawyer consults his books, but none finds a law to apply to the situation. Raj-Singh in each conversation indicates the passage of time and the long distance he has traveled seeking help. Finally, tired and weary after his weeks of search, he reaches the last lawyer in the fourth village and again states his problem. After a search through many books, the lawyer with a smile points to one page, and Raj-Singh reads the law written there: "If a place of worship is erected and standing, no one may tear it down. But it must be finished before the protection of the law is upon it."

Raj-Singh says, "This is the law I sought. We will build the church at night, and when it is finished, it cannot be torn down."

Scene IV: In the clearing. Time is after midnight

The painted background shows the completed rear wall of the church with the design of a cross cut out so that a light placed behind it will shine through. People are working as the scene opens, but there is not a sound. Finally, the wise old woman speaks to the workers: "We need to be more secret than the snake in the grass, and more busy than the tiger when he hunts food, and wise as the ant folk who have a task for each and keep each one working every minute."

The work continues with only an occasional whisper.
Some workers tramp down the floor.
Some measure the space.
Some carry bricks for side walls.
Some lay bricks in place.
Children bring water to workers.
Mothers watch sleeping children on mats nearby.

Finally when the work is finished, a dim light appears through the cross design of the rear wall. It is the sunrise of a new day. All the people gather inside the church wall and sit on the earthen floor.

Raj-Singh lifts his arms, and the heads of the people bow in prayer. . . .

Then the dramatic appearance of the Hindu priest and the landlord.

And the dramatic closing as the landlord tells the Christians, "Be secure. The hand of no man shall be lifted to move one brick from the wall nor injure in any way this house of worship. It is the law."

Raj-Singh declares, "We have built a house of worship for our God."

The landlord shrugs his shoulders. "I was fearful," he says, "of just one thing. I was afraid you might find out about that law. Even so, no idea came into my head that you might so greatly desire a house of God that you would work thus all night."

Bibliography

RESOURCE BOOKS

Andrews, Gladys. *Creative Rhythmic Movement for Children*. New York, Prentice-Hall, 1954.

Batcheller, Marjorie Hope. *Hand-and-Rod Puppets*. Columbus, Ohio State University Press, 1947.

———. *The Puppet Theatre Handbook*. New York, Harper & Brothers, 1947.

Brown, Corinne. *Creative Drama in the Lower School*. New York, Appleton-Century, 1930.

Brown, Jeanette Perkins. *The Storyteller in Religious Education*. Boston, The Pilgrim Press, 1951.

Burger, Isabel. *Creative Play Acting*. New York, A. S. Barnes, 1950.

Bryant, Sara Cone. *How to Tell Stories to Children*. New York, Houghton Mifflin Co., 1924.

Carter, Jean, and Ogden, Jesse. *The Play Book*. New York, Harcourt, Brace & Co., 1937.

De Witt, Marguerite E. *Let Us Recite Together*. Magnolia, Mass., Expression Co., 1935.

Durland, Frances Caldwell. *Creative Dramatics for Children*. Yellow Springs, Ohio, Antioch Press, 1952.

Flexner, M. W. *Hand Puppets*. New York, Samuel French, 1935.

Gullan, Marjorie. *Poetry Speaking for Children*. London, Methuen, 1950.

Hamm, Agnes Curran. *Choral Speaking Technique*. Milwaukee, Tower Press, 1951.

Jones, Robert Edmond. *The Dramatic Imagination*. New York, Duell, Sloan & Pearce, 1941.

Keppie, Elizabeth E. *Teaching of Choric Speech*. Magnolia, Mass., Expression Co., 1932.

Lease, Ruth, and Siks, G. B. *Creative Dramatics in Home, School, and Community*. New York, Harper & Brothers, 1952.

Lobingier, E. E. *Dramatization of Bible Stories*. Chicago, University of Chicago Press, 1918.

Mills, Winifred H. *Marionettes, Masks, and Shadows*. New York, Doubleday, 1927.

Mitchell, Elmer D., and Mason, S. *The Theory of Play*. New York, A. S. Barnes, revised 1948.

Overton, Grace Sloan. *Drama in Education*. New York, The Century Co., 1926.

Sawyer, Ruth. *The Way of the Storyteller*. New York, The Viking Press, 1942.

Shedlock, Marie. *The Art of the Story-Teller*. New York, Dover Publishers, 1952.

Sheehy, Emma D. *There's Music in Children*. New York, Henry Holt, 1952.

Shields, Elizabeth McE. *Music in the Religious Growth of Children*. Nashville, Abingdon-Cokesbury Press, 1943.

Soifer, Margaret K. *With Puppets, Mimes, and Shadows*. New York, The Furrow Press, 1936.

Thomas, Edith Lovell. *Music in Christian Education*. Nashville, Abingdon-Cokesbury Press, 1953.

Ward, Winifred. *Playmaking with Children*. New York, Appleton-Century-Crofts, 1947.

Willcox, Helen L. *Bible Study Through Educational Dramatics*. Nashville, Abingdon Press, 1924.

SONG AND WORSHIP BOOKS

Sing, Children, Sing, by Edith Lovell Thomas. Nashville, Abingdon-Cokesbury Press, 1939.

Hymns for Primary Worship. Philadelphia, The Westminster Press, 1946.

Hymns for Junior Worship. Philadelphia, The Westminster Press, 1940.

Songs for Little Children. United Church of Canada. Toronto, Ryerson Press, 1937.

Children's Worship in the Church School, by Jeanette E. Perkins. New York, Harper & Brothers, 1939.

More Children's Worship in the Church School, by Jeanette Perkins Brown. New York, Harper & Brothers, 1953.

Roads to Christmas, by Elizabeth Allstrom. Boston, The Pilgrim Press, 1951.

BIBLIOGRAPHY

FRIENDSHIP PRESS BOOKS

Many Hands in Many Lands, by Alice Geer Kelsey. 1953.
    "The Witch Doctor's Daughter"
    "By the Side of the Trail"
    "Within the Four Seas"
    "A Stick Rubs on Paper"
    "Omen and the Jumbies"
    "On Mars Hill"
    "The Independent Hen"
    "Only a Stable"
The Missionary Story Hour, edited by Nina Millen. 1952.
    "Zuka Changes His Mind"
    "The Boy in the Truck"
    "The Secret Cup"
    "The Gift of a Song"
    "From Nobody to Somebody"
    "Eyes for Tata Luis"
    "The Miracle"
    "One Stone and Another"
    "The Road to Friendship"
    "Making Men Over"
    "Fight or Shake Hands"
    "The Easter Song"
    "The Tanbark Church"
    "Ramón's Hat"
    "Come to Christmas"
    "The Congo Wise Man"
Blueberry Acres, by Alice Geer Kelsey. 1949.
    "Good-by to the Ozarks"
    "The Calico Cat"
    "Better Than the Dream"
The Whole World Singing, by Edith Lovell Thomas. 1950.
The Round Window, by Elizabeth Allstrom. 1953.
    "The Mischief Maker"
    "A Chance for School"
    "Two Bright Eyes"
    "The Three Surprises"
    "The Palm Sunday Play"
    "Peanuts for Church"

Rosita: a Little Girl of Puerto Rico, by Jeanette Perkins Brown. 1948.
Children and Their Toys Around the World. Text by Nina Millen, pictures by Janet Smalley. 1954.
    "Ahmed's Pipes"
    "Shu Chin's Kite"
    "Shanti and Prem Look for Toys"
Children at Worship Around the World. Text by Nina Millen, pictures by Janet Smalley. 1954.
    "A Place of Beauty"
    "Thanks for Food"
    "Gifts for the World's Children"
    "Bedtime Prayer"
    "A Song of Praise"
Children and Their Homes Around the World. Text by Nina Millen, pictures by Janet Smalley. 1956.
    "Putting Up New Year Greetings"
    "Caring for the Harvest"
    "Making Ready for Christmas"
    "Hanging the Christmas Wreath"
World Friends: Spreading the Gospel. Text by Elizabeth Allstrom. 1955.
    "The Teacher Points to the Words"
    "What Does the Picture Say?"
    "I Will Sing to the Lord"
    "A Church on Wheels"
Manuel: a Little Boy of Mexico, by Jeanette Perkins Brown. 1951.
Stories of the Book of Books, by Grace W. McGavran. 1947.
    "White Sails and Blue Sea"
    "A Miner Strikes Pay Dirt"
    "Follow the Line"
    "Seven Pieces of Silk"
    "The Prize Bible"
    "The Dusted Bible"
    "Ships"
The Singing Secret, by Elizabeth Allstrom. 1955.
    "The Singing Secret"
    "God's Gift to Paquito"
    "Sadao and the Story Man"
Nezbah's Lamb, by Edith J. Agnew. 1954.
Keiko's Birthday, by Jeanette Perkins Brown. 1954.

BIBLIOGRAPHY

Bright Pathways, by Esma Rideout Booth. 1955.
    "Friend in the North"
We Gather Together, by Grace W. McGavran. 1951.
    "The Old Story in a New Land"
    "The Church That Was Builded by Moonlight"
Sidewalk Kids, by Gertrude Jenness Rinden. 1954.
    "Story Girl"
    "One World for Johnny"
    "New Hands"
The Boy with the Busy Walk, by Anne M. Halladay. 1954.
    "The 'Borrowed' Camp"
Chand of India, by Irene Mason Harper. 1954.
    "Visit from a Cobra"
Second Son, by Margaret Clemens McDowell. 1956.
    "My Nipa Hut"
    "Market Day"
Ricardo's Search, by Grace W. McGavran. 1956.
    "The Search Is Ended"
The Gray Eyes Family, by Edith J. Agnew. 1952.
Juan and Juanita, by Sara G. Klein. 1956.
The Three Camels, by Elsa Helena Spriggs. 1951.
Children's Games from Many Lands, edited by Nina Millen. 1943.
Here's How and When, by Armilda B. Keiser. 1952.

> A new book, *Missionary Stories to Play and Tell,* will be available in 1958. It includes many of the missionary stories recommended in this book, with the exception of those already contained in the previously published collection, *The Missionary Story Hour.*

Index

162

INDEX

INDEX

A WORD ABOUT THE FORMAT

The text of this book is set in linotype Fairfield, the first type face from the hand of the distinguished American artist and engraver, Rudolph Ruzicka. A master craftsman whose talent has long been dedicated to clarity, he has given his type face a trim grace and virility, coupled with a spirited design and sensitive balance.

Composed by: Ruttle, Shaw & Wetherill, Inc., Philadelphia · Text, jackets, and paper covers by: Affiliated Lithographers, Inc., New York · Binding by: Book Craftsmen Associates, Inc., New York · Text Paper: Warren's Bookman Offset Wove.

Typographic design by Margery W. Smith
Binding by Louise E. Jefferson